HACKERS AND HEROES

How Everyone Can Participate in the Tech Economy

HACKERS AND HEROES

How Everyone Can Participate in the Tech Economy

SRAVAN ANKARAJU

Divergence Press

ISBN: Paperback 978-1-7377761-0-9

eISBN: 978-1-7377761-1-6

Cover image by: Liu Zishan/Shutterstock.com

Book design by Katinka de Ruiter

First printing edition 2021

Divergence Press

14665 Midway Road

Suite 220

Addison, TX 75001

https://divergence.press

For Sangeeta, my companion
on the information superhighway.
non clamor sed amor.

Contents

CHAPTER ONE

Hope Is Not a Strategy

An analysis of the history of technology shows that technological change is exponential, contrary to the common-sense "intuitive linear" view. So we won't experience 100 years of progress in the 21st century—it will be more like 20,000 years of progress (at today's rate). The "returns," such as chip speed and cost-effectiveness, also increase exponentially. There's even exponential growth in the rate of exponential growth. Within a few decades, machine intelligence will surpass human intelligence, leading to The Singularity—technological change so rapid and profound it represents a rupture in the fabric of human history. The implications include the merger of biological and nonbiological intelligence, immortal software-based humans, and ultra-high levels of intelligence that expand outward in the universe at the speed of light.

Ray Kurzweil, "The Law of Accelerating Returns," Essays, Kurzweil: Tracking the acceleration of intelligence [March 7, 2001]

One machine can do the work of fifty ordinary men. No machine can do the work of one extraordinary man.

Elbert Hubbard, A Thousand and One Epigrams, 1911.

AI.

Blockchain.

Quantum computing.

Genetic editing.

Human machine interface.

Not too long ago, these words left most people scratching their heads and wondering if they had stumbled upon something pulled from science fiction. Now, in the early decades of the twenty-first century, these enabling technologies have evolved and continue to evolve at such an exponential rate that they are effecting unprecedented change across the globe and in nearly every industry. The Industrial Revolution that swept the twentieth century into the modern age will be eclipsed by the technological age that's underway right now.

In one example, bankers are being replaced by robots to complete basic data processing and calculations. JP Morgan Chase & Co. quietly laid off 140 employees and replaced them with robots—and that was in 2016. Just last year, the bank set up more robots whose job was to ensure that its remaining bankers weren't fudging expense reports.[1]

A biotechnology company called Karius recently announced

that it had developed a machine that can isolate and sequence DNA and provide results within 24 hours of taking a patient sample, relieving clinical microbiologists of one of their elemental duties—one that requires nearly a decade of education and training.[2]

And in the midst of the coronavirus pandemic in 2020, businesses increasingly turned to software and other technologies that can automate rote clerical tasks as well as more complex activities like reading and analyzing PDFs and cataloguing materials.

To put that in perspective, consider that approximately 400,000 jobs were lost to automation between 1990 to 2007. In the middle of March 2020—the height of the pandemic in the United States—40 million jobs evaporated. True, some of those jobs came back as the country reopened, but economists at places like the Massachusetts Institute of Technology (MIT) and Boston University estimate that over 40 percent of those jobs—from cashiers and security guards to customer-service representatives and bank tellers—may be lost to robots and AI for good.[3] And the kinds of jobs that are disappearing are not just the low-hanging fruit of the blue collar and service sectors; every industry is experiencing the gut-punch of massive change, seemingly overnight.

Those most impacted right now are women and minorities, while, at least in the short term, higher-wage-earning professionals and those employed by so-called "superstar" companies like Amazon and Google may feel as though their jobs are safe, but the rapid nature of technological advancement has demonstrated that it's only a matter of time before those positions are threatened, too.

Ready to bury your head in the sand? Though tempting, I'm sure, all is not lost. Remember, though the Industrial Revolution eliminated rural farm jobs, those farmers did not simply stop working; they found new jobs in the new economy. The same is true now. Innovation is good—history has proven that to us, and it can continue to be a boon to the global workforce. The question is how to navigate this brave new world. Where does all this massive change leave the average worker?

As the old saying goes, If you can't beat 'em, join 'em. What I mean by that is, rather than throw your hands up in despair every time you read a story about how AI is taking away jobs, why not figure out a way to be part of that revolution? To that end, workers must be willing to retool and adapt to a workplace that is going to be in a constant state of change. The pace of innovation will render jobs obsolete at a regular clip—that's simply the new reality we have to accept if we're going to succeed.

All well and good, you may think, but how can someone possibly pivot for a job that may not yet even exist? Some of those "jobs of the future" are already here, and a willingness to learn the necessary skills and think outside the box will put some workers more than a few steps ahead of their peers. To do that will require agility and responsiveness as well as being fluent in the language of the digital world. That's why I launched Divergence Academy: to empower individuals to not merely survive, but to thrive in the high-speed tech and data-driven economy. Emerging technology can't run itself; it needs living, breathing human beings to keep it running. That means preparing for careers in AI, cloud computing, cybersecurity, statistical analysis and data science. Think of Divergence as a vocational school for the 21st century—hands on practice with real-time feedback and apprenticeship opportunities in tech-driven industries.

But that's not me, you may be thinking to yourself. Perhaps you're a war veteran or a stay-at-home mom ready to reenter the workforce. *I'm not right for this kind of job,* you think.

I respectfully disagree.

Anyone with the right focus and drive can participate in the tech economy.

It just takes a willingness to diverge from the traditional and the predictable.

I am living proof that what it takes is achievable to anyone.

As a teenager in India, especially one coming of age in the mid-1980s, it was expected that I would become a doctor or an engineer—that was just what everyone from my town in my age group did.

I became neither.

In fact, I knew as soon as I opened the envelope containing my college admission test results that I would need to figure something else out; I did so poorly on my engineering entrance exam that I had zero hope of getting accepted into a high-quality engineering program. Here I was, a nineteen-year-old who'd already failed his first attempt at finding his path in life—I needed a plan B, stat. I couldn't dawdle. I had to act.

With medical school and engineering school effectively tossed from the scope of possibilities, I didn't panic.

To paraphrase Robert Frost, I took the path less traveled, and, yes, it has made all the difference. By charting my own course and trusting my instincts, I discovered I had a deep affinity for working with computers. I had always enjoyed tinkering—taking things apart, seeing how they worked, and putting them back together—but in India, that wasn't always possible. You had few choices: go to school, become a white-collar professional, and accept your destiny as it came to you. That wasn't going to cut it for me. In fact, by following a non-traditional career path—one that I carved out for myself—I eventually joined the inner sanctum of Microsoft.

In many ways, that's where I feel my journey truly began. I started my Microsoft career as a senior consultant in technology integration in January 2001. I stayed there for nearly fourteen years before once again finding myself at a crossroads. But, as I will demonstrate in the pages to come, getting there wasn't easy: we make our own luck, after all, and I learned plenty along the way.

You Have to Do the Work

Let's back up to that moment when I realized that I was facing the great unknown after receiving the crushing news of my lousy exam results. It should come as no surprise that the best colleges only wanted students with the best test scores, and I knew that it wasn't worth my time to try and enroll at a lesser school—even if I might learn something about engineering. A degree from one of those institutions would have been worthless. With engineering closed to me, I enrolled in a three-year bachelor's degree program focused on math, physics, chemistry, and the general sciences. This was a solid start, but I knew I needed to do more—to specialize—in order to build a successful career. But in what? Even in the 1980s, it was clear that the future was in computers, and so while I was an undergraduate, I also enrolled in an institute called Apple (not the same as the iPhone creators), which was accredited by the National Computing Centre (NCC) in the United Kingdom and offered classes in software engineering.

Even as I was hitting the books at two institutions, I had to work to pay for all this education. I landed my first IT-related job when I was nineteen, working at Citation Computer Consultants. I spent my days in the classroom, and then I would go to work in the evenings after classes let out, from five to nine o'clock at night. Then, I'd head back home and prepare for the next day. The pace was breakneck, but I discovered that I could handle it—in fact, even today, I am at my best when my days are full.

I'd be lying if I said it wasn't exhausting, but this combination of work and education accelerated my learning and my depth of understanding in the field. Further, it was during this time that I fell truly, madly, deeply in love with computers. I might not have been cut out for studying and acing exam after exam. But I didn't need to be. I could tinker and play around with things. I could learn the technology and put it to work. Forget theory—leave that to the academics. I wanted to create. To take complicated pieces of equipment and make them hum. If I spent enough time figuring out how things worked on a practical level, I could make magic.

Time flies when you don't have a minute to take notice of what is around you. Soon enough, I was done with school and facing another turning point. Now I realized that not only did I love working with computers, I had an itch to manage others. I had already tasted what it was like to lead a team at my part-time IT job, and I wanted to learn more. I decided to look beyond the borders of my home country and set my sights on Australia.

Why Australia? In India, as in many other countries, there are agencies that help young people pursue higher education. I paid 10,000 rupees—about $400 in U.S. dollars at the time—to an agency to help me land at a school in Australia. Look, 10,000 rupees may not sound like much, but I was asking for a significant investment from my mother at the time. Well, guess what happened? I didn't get into that program. My mother's savings went down the drain.

Now what?

I hauled myself down to the student placement agency and asked what my next move should be. The Australian master's program had rejected me, but there were still options—how did I feel about going to the United States? It turned out that the University of Central Oklahoma was ready to welcome me as a matriculating master's in business administration (MBA) candidate—all I needed was to take a few hours of prerequisites, which I flew through. By the fall of 1991, I was on a plane bound for the Show Me State, and believe me, I was ready to show them that I could meet whatever tasks they put in front of me.

Remember, opportunities are everywhere, you've got to be curious and willing to seek them out. And hungry to put in the work.

Learning Curves

If you threw a dart at a map of Oklahoma and it landed dead center, you'd hit Edmond, where the University of Central Oklahoma is located. The city is the fifth largest in the state, and located along iconic Route 66, directly in the central lane of Tornado Alley. I had never experienced tornadoes back home, and I wasn't sure I'd survive my first one. But soon enough, I had the procedures down pat and was prepared to bunker down at a moment's notice whenever I heard those ear-piercing sirens sounding the alarm.

Fans of the Olympics may recall that one of America's most decorated gymnasts, Shannon Miller, hails from Edmond, and the city was named one of *Newsmax*'s "Top 25 Most Uniquely American Cities and Towns." With its beauty pageants, fireworks on the Fourth of July, and yes, a Main Street, I had left India and landed right in the middle of the American Promise.

To fully partake in the American way of life, though, I needed a driver's license. I passed *that* test, I'm pleased to report, with no problem—except that my ID card also read in large font "UNDER 21" which didn't help my social life too much. Not that I had much time to consider extracurriculars, anyway.

While I was pursuing my MBA, I worked to pay the bills, just like I had at home. I swept the university floors and scrubbed the toilets as a janitor, washed dishes in the university mess hall, and mowed the green quad to a perfect two-and-half-inch height. I even took a job at the local Taco Bell, where I got my first taste of management for the princely sum of $4.25 an hour.

Did I mention I was already engaged, too?

You Can't Do It Alone

Sangeeta was my beloved from back home. Our mothers had both been schoolteachers and close friends. We lived a few blocks from each other growing up, and Sangeeta used to come over my house and watch VHS tapes after school. We always seemed to be running into each other and hanging out with large groups of friends. Ours wasn't a traditional courtship dictated by our families—rather, our love grew organically. I liked her when we both lived in India, and we maintained a long-distance courtship for a while, but it wasn't until I had spent a year stateside that I realized at the ripe old age of nineteen how important she was to my life and my happiness. I summoned the courage to ask her if she was ready to join me as my bride. One of my bargaining chips was that I wasn't intending to stay in America, only wanting to finish my education there, maybe get a few years of work experience under my belt, and then move somewhere else.

Sangeeta was working as a travel agent at the time, and I know taking time off from work to marry me and accompany me to Oklahoma was a huge commitment. Thankfully, in 1993 she said yes. We had a big wedding surrounded by our family, and at twenty-three years old I was married to the love of my life. We've been together ever since. Sangeeta is my partner in life and in work. She's been right there with me through it all. Work and life simply blended together, with us as a team. In the mornings, she and I would have breakfast together, then go our separate ways. Sangeeta loved baking and when a position at a cute local bakery shop opened up, she jumped at the opportunity to help boost our bottom line.

Neither of us thought we'd stay in the United States for long. By January 1994, we were situated in our little apartment in Edmond, fully prepared for a few years of life in the heartland. All of our furniture was secondhand, and we didn't put much effort into making friends or putting down roots. Our first snowfall in Oklahoma—all four inches of it—reminded us just how far from home we were. But we had each other.

We developed a rhythm that suited us. After school or work, well after the sun had set, I'd come home and start pulling a computer apart, even if it was close to midnight. I'd tinker with it, trying to see how things fit together. Sangeeta was right there next to me, eating noodles and handing me pliers, screwdrivers, and any other tool I needed. She always knew what I was looking for and where to find it if I didn't.

Sangeeta demonstrated enormous patience while I was in school. Summer commuter hours were hectic, usually beginning around 5:15 p.m. and ending well after ten o'clock. My work hours were a nightmare—I opened at McDonald's on a shift from 4:00 a.m. until 2:00 p.m., and closed a Taco Bell shift from 10:00 p.m. until 4:00 a.m. The locations were across the street from each other which helped me plan consecutive shifts. I was physically exhausted and slept sporadically. Sangeeta remained my steadfast champion throughout. She has always been my partner, my sounding board, and, if I'm being totally honest, the real CEO behind everything I've built. I couldn't have gotten through school or anything else in my life without her.

I graduated in 1994, but open management positions, especially for an immigrant in need of employment sponsorship, were few and far between to me, even with an MBA in hand. Plus, I still had to think about my H1B visa and maintaining my green card status. By then, Sangeeta and I had decided that we wanted to stay in the United States, so I chose the path of least resistance and applied for two jobs: one at the telecommunications company MCI, and another with the Kansas Department of Transportation. Before I heard back from MCI, the hiring manager at KDOT asked if I could come in. I remember making the five-hour drive to Topeka for my interview. The manager wanted to hire me on the spot.

"What's your compensation range?" he asked me.

"Well, considering my experience, I'd be happy with anything between $30,000 to $36,000."

Of course, the KDOT rep offered me $30,000.

I said I'd think about it—I had my interview with MCI the

next day.

In a nearly identical situation, I was offered the position and asked the same question. This time I knew how the game was played.

"Well, considering my experience, I'd be happy with anything between $36,000 and $39,000."

Of course, MCI offered me $36,000.

The next day, I called KDOT and told them about the offer from MCI.

"Why didn't you tell us you wanted $36,000?" the hiring manager asked. "We thought you would be happy."

Lesson learned—ask for what you really want. You may be surprised.

And with that, we bid Edmond farewell and packed our bags and headed for Colorado Springs, Colorado, where my new office was located. Sangeeta and I were expecting our time in Colorado to be brief, but to our happy surprise, there was a large Indian community that welcomed us heartily. Many also worked at MCI. In what seemed like an instant, we had a network of new friends and a full social calendar. Though Sangeeta and I loved Oklahoma—there's no place quite like it in terms of its character and hospitality—Colorado felt like home.

Tinker Tailor Data Boy

My first major project involved figuring out how to ensure data could flow uninterrupted from system to system. I always managed to hack together a solution, and management noticed. The next thing I knew, I was handed software integration project after software integration project. Eventually I was given one assignment that was so difficult that I had to buy my own computer to break apart in order to figure out the problem. Sangeeta and I went to Dillard's department store on a Friday night, where I maxed out my credit card to the astronomical tune of two thousand dollars to buy a computer.

I spent the next 48 hours breaking, hacking, and repairing the machine. By Monday morning, I went to see my supervisors and said, "I have something for you to see." I had solved the problem. And no, MCI never compensated me for my purchase.

Not only had I solved the problem, but my supervisors wanted me to explain to a dozen or so other C-suite executives how I had done it. There I was, a 24-year-old immigrant explaining the solution to seasoned supervisors. It was surreal.

Next thing I knew, I was working on the coolest, most innovative projects MCI had on deck. At one point, it seemed I was doing a little too well.

"Sravan, you're wrapping these projects up too quickly," my supervisor said. "Are you bored?"

"Hardly," I responded. "Give me more."

Ask and you shall receive. Almost overnight, I was assigned to two different groups to streamline their projects. One was an application built on Windows NT and the Microsoft Foundation Class Library; another was True64 Unix. By 1996 I went from $36,000 to

$50,000 per year. I was a long way from slinging burritos at Taco Bell. I felt invincible.

I still wanted more, though.

So I found another client, a company called Monitor Labs. I worked with them to build their database systems so that they could support a complete rewrite of an environmental pollution monitoring system. While there, I became acquainted with the CEO, Scott Harrison. He started out as a mentor and soon became a family friend. We're still close to this day.

Nevertheless, I continued to feel this urge to find new things to do.

Between all this, my son, Mayank, was born on September 25th, 1998.

My household was a busy one, but it was full of happiness. Luckily, we had an ever-expanding network of friends near us in Colorado, and Sangeeta's family dotted the American landscape, with an aunt in Buffalo, a cousin in Minneapolis, more cousins in New York. When the stress of caring for a newborn felt all-encompassing, it was mighty soothing to know we had a support system a phone call away. We also made time to travel to see our family—long car trips crisscrossing the country offered amazing opportunities to fully appreciate the vast breadth and beauty of the United States.

Now that I also had a child to care for, I did all kinds of jobs, spending evenings and my free time doing whatever work I could find—systems integration, consulting, freelance work—which prompted me to start my own company, Cilium Interactive Networks. I was moonlighting as a systems integration consultant, getting freelance work wherever I could.

Starting Cilium was such an interesting experience. It took time to determine the perfect name to represent the brand. Paramecium, Cilia, and Web were also under consideration. At the time, the world wide web was only operating on version two or three. In the budding age of technology, we wanted to be intentional with our name choice and after much debate, finally landed on Cilium Interactive Networks.

I no longer own Cilium, but the lessons I gleaned as its founder have stuck with me: staying curious and staying hungry for more knowledge and more work will help lead to success, no matter what the industry demands. Back then, you were not an entrepreneur, you were just helping a friend out. You were coming to the table with a new perspective and offering free hands to collaborate, and you never shirked an opportunity to try something out of the box.

Meanwhile, I was keeping the lights on over at Monitor Labs, but it was becoming increasingly clear that I was outgrowing the position. Specifically, I realized that I wanted to learn and build next-generation software. To do that, I needed to know more about Microsoft technologies. I decided to take some classes and soon became an expert at the technology. I decided to apply for a job at a place called Raymond James Consulting Company—which later became British Telecom IT Services Organization—not to be confused with the Florida-based Raymond James Financial

Institution. I became the architect for a company they were creating called Open Financial Solutions—a consortium of five credit unions that built home banking and bill payment solutions. This was 1999 and one of the earliest forays into online banking, right during the global fears of Y2K. I was thrilled to be at the vanguard of this emerging opportunity.

When this task was completed, I was sent across the United States to help other institutions launch their various online and tech-based business development. It was heady stuff, but I was starting to get tired of all the travel—I missed my family, plus all the consulting work had taken me away from my first love, which was getting elbow-deep in the rich soil of the technology itself.

Once again, I polished my application and looked beyond the horizon.

Demonstrate Your Worth. But Be Patient.

To get to the future, you have to do a good job in the present. You need to take care of your life *today,* your family *today,* your customers *today,* so that you are set up for future success. It's not necessarily easy—in fact, I'd say be prepared to do just about anything necessary to make it work.

But patience is also key. It's easy to lose sight of your end goal or to feel overwhelmed thinking of the enormity of it all. Focus on the situation in front of you. Do the best you can, and doors will open.

Many new business owners want to turn a profit fast—who wouldn't? However, process must come before product. An effective, streamlined, consistent process has been the key to all my long-term gains. When I feel the temptation to speed up, I mindfully practice the art of slowing down. I simplify. This is optimal for everyone involved, especially since I naturally want to go at lightspeed. We *all* need a little bit of breathing room while learning. We *all* need to be operating in tandem to reach a common goal. For my sanity, for the sake of my team and the success of my business, I make sure that I am always focusing on the most important task at hand. Success is about presence and patience.

CHAPTER TWO

The Microsoft Years

With all the abundance we have of computers and computing, what is scarce is human attention and time.

Satya Nadella, CEO, Microsoft

Almost all our misfortunes in life come from the wrong notions we have about the things that happen to us. To know men thoroughly, to judge events sanely is, therefore, a great step towards happiness.

Stendhal (Henri Beyle) Journal [December 10, 1801]

Those of us of a certain age remember where we were when the threat of impending digital disaster loomed over the world. It was 1999, and computer experts were sounding an alarm that our "over-reliance" on digital technology would be society's downfall. With the stroke of midnight on January 1, 2000, streetlights would no longer function, trains would careen off their tracks, banks would lose millions of dollars, and even, perhaps, top-secret nuclear codes themselves would suddenly become open knowledge.

Our forthcoming doom was imminent.

There was a growing sense of panic, with media outlets breathlessly and relentlessly fueling rumors of global economic collapse. This fear was stoked by the unprecedented potential failure of worldwide computer systems caused by a widely used piece of code that told computers how to recognize years.

In fact, "Y2K," as the event came to be called, was the result of a bunch of computer programmers looking for a shortcut. Rather than list years as four digits, programmers cut the year in half, stringing years in code as the last two digits only. Time saving, yes, but also shortsighted: billions of microprocessors around the world had been produced over a thirty-year period with two-digit year dates. The anticipated crash would occur if computers failed to differentiate the year 2000 from 1900. If this did happen, the consequences for nearly every facet of the global economy could indeed be catastrophic. Most mere mortals steeled themselves for the worst, but in reality governments and private organizations had been aware of the issue for years, pouring billions of dollars into creating patches and workarounds to avert a digital meltdown.[1]

As one millennium gave way to another, people around the world breathed a collective sigh of relief as reports of minimal glitches, rather than the hyped-up possibility of international disaster, made news. In fact, Y2K had benefited the technology industry in two ways. First, the crisis revealed just how important IT had become to most industries, not just those based in Silicon Valley. Executives at brick-and-mortars like Home Depot and Exxon got an up-close tutorial on how digital technologies were utilized for everything from ordering to fulfillment. Second, though Y2K became a widespread concern, the issue was quickly remedied once identified. In fact, some firms had been on the Y2K case since at least 1995, according to the U.S. Department of Commerce.

Though the issue was relatively easy to correct once discovered, it came at a cost: businesses and government agencies were estimated to have spent $100 billion just for this purpose.[2] "Because the problem has been widely recognized, private firms and governments have had real incentives to fix their problems—which in turn is the primary reason why Y2K does not now appear to pose a real economic threat," explained the U.S. Department of Commerce's November 1999 assessment of the phenomenon. In short, Y2K ultimately proved to be more media hype than substance, but if firms hadn't addressed the situation, it could have easily gotten bad very quickly—without IT professionals, this would have been a painful moment in our history. Y2K illustrated just how essential IT programmers have become to the workforce.

Through all of this, I was still working at Monitor Labs, which did not experience any Y2K-related snafus. I had recently dusted off my resume and was ready to try something new, particularly within the realm of next-generation software. The work being done with Microsoft technology piqued my interest, and I decided it was time to enroll in courses that would amplify my understanding of new concepts. After working with Raymond James to build their online banking systems—hardly revolutionary today, but in the 2000s, online banking was a new concept—I was approached by Cotelligent to consider a senior position that focused on online business development. I accepted the opportunity to travel the country building the firm's growing consulting service arm. It still amazes me to see just how far we've come in two decades: once upon a time, most of us would have voluntarily eaten snakes rather than share our banking information online. Now look at us! I was able to get my hands in the dirt at the ground level, so to speak, and the opportunity was phenomenal.

Between 1999 and 2000 my hourly pay increased from $50 per hour to $85 per hour. This was a significant raise and a great boon to my family. Meanwhile, I had not yet received my green card, but employment laws were more lenient back then. I was able to transition between contracts and Cotelligent was willing to wait for my green card paperwork to make its way through seemingly endless miles of red tape.

After a few years of building online commerce solutions, I realized I missed tinkering with technology. I determined it was best for me to start seeking alternate opportunities. I applied to Microsoft, then considered the Valhalla of the computer world. Shortly after, I was offered a position with Microsoft Consulting Services, with California or Denver as my home base and a compensation package of around $110,000 per year as my base salary, plus another $20,000 in bonuses and other options. At either location, I would be tasked with building system solutions for major Microsoft clients like Amtrak and Adecco, and Applied Material. Though

Silicon Valley beckoned, I opted for the Denver location—no need to relocate—and was hoping for the best when I was met with the news that my green card application had been rejected.

While I was applying for the position at Microsoft, Pittsburgh Business Consultants was acquired by IT consulting firm Cotelligent, which did not update Immigration and Naturalization Services about the change of the company's name, thereby rendering my paperwork inaccurate. My employment locale thus indeterminable, the government paper pushers handling my application enforced a strict stop-work order, which in turn delayed my moving forward with Microsoft. Thankfully, Microsoft brass proved to be quite generous and agreed to wait while I sorted everything out.

Of course, the adage of "hurry up and wait" applies here. While waiting for my revised application to wind its way through the system, I decided to return home to India to visit family I hadn't seen in years. I stayed in contact with Microsoft throughout my travels and solidified a start date in January of 2001. They were patient throughout the entire seven-month hold-up. Though I had gone back to India in 1996, I took a few months now to go to Hyderabad and show off Mayank to my family. I saw my brother, who had gotten married the year prior, my sister, and of course, my parents. In my absence, the middle class had exploded in growth, largely due to the booming tech sector that had built up in and around Hyderabad—locals have even nicknamed it "Cyberabad" as a result. It was a wonderful, restorative trip, the kind you don't realize you need until you've reached your destination.

By the time I returned, the doors were opened, and I was a Microsoft man.

It appeared that my non-traditional path was bearing fruit. I remained confident that each step I took would lead to another level, even if I still didn't know what that level held in store. And I realized that nothing is wasted—every place I worked and everyone I met would one day fuel my entrepreneurial dreams in the greater technology ecosystem.

Don't Leave Your Value on the Table

I was no longer a solo star when I arrived at Microsoft, but a member of an A-list rock group. Being surrounded by the industry's biggest and brightest proved to be a learning curve all its own. To employ another cliché, we were *all* big fish. It was difficult, at a place like Microsoft, to be transcendent. Everyone seemed to be within spitting distance of conjuring up the next great world-saving solution. I fought down my desire to steal the show and instead focused on giving my best. The first month demonstrated just how much Microsoft would require of me.

My initial project was a four-month initiative for a telecom company called Global Crossing, which involved building online systems for managing and tracking expenses. Global Crossing wasn't in Colorado, however, but on the other end of the country in New Jersey. I became the Marathon Man of the friendly skies. On Monday mornings I would leave for the Denver airport in the predawn hours to make a six o'clock flight. I arrived in New Jersey by ten, then commuted one hour to Parsippany where I'd work through Thursday. Then, I returned home and prepared to do it all again a few days later. Meanwhile, I developed a penchant for marketing. I learned how to engage groups of people and how to provide elegant, versatile solutions for complex situations.

I was thriving at Microsoft—too bad my superiors didn't know that. It was not until I received my first review that I felt deflated. My boss invited me into his office, where he broke down the metrics of success at Microsoft. Basically, the company employed an inverted ranking system, with five as the highest, three was average, and one was poor. Scoring a three means that you have to pay more attention to your performance. I earned threes across the board. Employees were rewarded through stocks and bonuses. I received neither bonus—a reward for past performance—nor an investment in my future in the form of stock. This communicated both that my present efforts were inadequate and that I was not predicted to be a major contributor to the future of Microsoft. Understandably, I was not pleased to hear this.

"I know you're killing yourself and having great success on your projects, but we need to *see* it," he said.

"What do I have to do to turn this around?" I asked.

"Start sharing," my boss responded. "Be bold. Be confident. Share like you mean it."

This is an across-the-board concept in business. Basically, corporate leaders need compelling narratives told with clear talking points to show *their* superiors who is pulling their weight in the office and who isn't. I hadn't been giving them enough talking points. At one point, my mentor, John Ano, advised the following, and it's stuck with me ever since:

"Give yourself the luxury to present among your peers."

I was three years into what I thought was top of my career, and I felt like I was failing in the eyes of my superiors. Thankfully, they extended an olive branch to set me up for success. And it worked; by September, I was asked to join the Microsoft Business Desktop Deployment Teams. The goal of the project was to build a team that would help firms transition to working on modern desktops. IT professionals were accustomed to change happening in massive waves, but now, technological progress was constant, requiring sustained adaptation which left some professionals overwhelmed. Desktop Deployment was created to ensure smooth transitions. This concept, that change was ever-present and would require continuous retooling, would come back to me when I started toying with the notion of building a school.

Meanwhile, Sangeeta and I had been in Highlands Ranch, Colorado since 1999 and were finally feeling like we had put down roots. This charming Denver residential suburb had everything going for it: gorgeous mountain views, nature trails, and excellent schools. When Trisha was born in October 2001, our family felt whole. Those bonds would soon be tested and strained to their limits.

In December of 2003, I was on a work trip in Redmond, Washington. In the middle of a meeting, I received a frantic call from

Sangeeta imploring me to come home. My five-year-old son Mayank had come down with a fever that would not break. Sangeeta rushed him to the hospital. On the way, she called my sister and brother-in-law who lived nearby so they could take care of Trisha while we sorted out what was happening with Mayank. Sangeeta's mother flew in from India, as did an aunt who worked as a physician in Buffalo. Thankfully, we were able to assemble a support team in rapid time, and we would rely on them tremendously in the months to come.

I flew home and met my family in the ER. Mayank had the flu, so we had to wait for him to clear that virus before the doctors could conclusively diagnose him. The doctors knew he suffered from a bacterial infection of some sort, and finally diagnosed him with bacterial endocarditis. Essentially, endocarditis is a bacterium that preys on the mitral valve in the heart and degrades its structure. For four days Mayank rested while his symptoms improved, but we were hardly in the clear. Microsoft could wait. I took a three month leave of absence to shepherd my son through his treatment and recovery.

Mayank's health remained precarious. Initially, the doctors told us he would not need surgery because they were confident his tissue would repair on its own. Several months of waiting showed little improvement. In fact, his heart began overcompensating for the leaking valve by growing too large, putting pressure on his lungs and ultimately leading to pulmonary hypertension. The doctors determined that five-year-old Mayank needed heart surgery.

In the midst of this, I returned to Microsoft.

My first project back was leading a Business Desktop Deployment workshop in Montréal. This was a headache for a multitude of reasons. First, there was a bit of a language barrier: I have an Indian accent, and I was leading a seminar full of people who primarily spoke French. Then, as mercilessly as before, fate stepped in. During another meeting, Sangeeta called. Mayank was scheduled for surgery that could not wait any longer, and it was imperative that I fly home.

Mayank's valve had torn apart under the stress of the bacterial infection. The physicians planned on suturing it, but when they saw the state of it, they realized it needed to be completely replaced. Thankfully, the doctors were prepared for this scenario and had already procured an artificial valve.

Mayank was in pain when he emerged from surgery. He was intubated and hooked up to several machines. He could not speak, and we strived to meet his needs as best we could. Sangeeta did a beautiful job at interpreting his silences. He would begin: "W-w," and she would rush for ice chips. *Water.* He wanted water, but he could not have fluids, as he had just come out of surgery.

It became evident that I had a decision to make. With Mayank's health so precarious, travelling around the country was no longer an option. Though I was hesitant to request that Microsoft keep my projects local, I saw no other option. Thankfully, my supervisors were understanding and placed me as a consultant with Lockheed Martin Business Solutions.

The system I developed launched Lockheed towards stratospheric success. In turn, they received an $8 billion contract from NASA for The Crew Exploration Vehicle, a project designed to shuttle humans to Mars. The collaborative business capture system (CBCS) I constructed locally made a universal impact.

Mayank's health began to improve and soon he started back to school. Everything about him has always been advanced. He was—and remains—emotionally intelligent and empathetic. His teachers noted that he was incredibly creative and socially adept. Early in the year they chose to advance him from kindergarten to first grade—confident he would thrive with a challenge. Sangeeta and I were both impressed and concerned by his tenaciousness. I would often think: *What if he falls? What if he bleeds? He's on blood thinners—what if they cannot stop the bleeding?* I had to detach from the scenarios over time and allow him to just be himself. He was a force to be reckoned with. Unfortunately, Mayank was so advanced that he was soon finding school boring.

Meanwhile, my daughter Trisha kept bringing home colds, as children generally do. Sangeeta and Trisha would rotate colds, leaving us constantly concerned for Mayank's safety. One summer, Sangeeta decided to try out a mini homeschooling experiment. Sangeeta began organizing courses—dissecting pig hearts, visiting a local museum, mapping out architectural plans for an imagined playground—as a trial run to see if homeschooling might be a better option. When summer came to an end, the children wanted nothing to do with going back to traditional school. Sangeeta could tailor the coursework precisely to the interests and needs of Mayank and Trisha, who were in fifth and second grade, respectively. And clearly, they were thriving. So, before the school year began, Sangeeta approached the elementary school principal to discuss options. The children were healthy and thriving academically. What was there to lose?

"I'm going to try this for a month and a half," Sangeeta told the principal. "Will there be a place for them if it doesn't work out?"

Amazingly, the principal agreed to hold two spots for the kids if homeschooling wasn't successful after a month and a half.

Sangeeta left the school and the kids never went back. And Mayank never fell sick once. That was all the proof that we needed.

This wasn't an excuse for the children to spend their days in their pajamas: Sangeeta carefully constructed the homeschooling program to focus on project-based learning and critical thinking. The state required us to submit Intent to Homeschool paperwork to the district, as well as details about the type of curriculum we were using. Everything had to pass muster with the Douglas County Department of Education. Sangeeta purchased various homeschool curricula and attended all the national homeschooling conferences. There was no one-size-fits-all approach, even for two children; Mayank always wanted to follow the precise outline in the book, while Trisha was more interested in doing hands-on projects.

At the time, homeschoolers represented about one percent of the overall school-age population. In 1999, approximately 850,000 students were homeschooled. By 2016, the number had grown to

1.7 million, and after the national experiment with learning from home in the spring of 2020, the National Home School Association anticipated that 10 percent of the school age population would not only choose to stay learning from home, but be homeschooled.[3] On a single day in July, the association received 3,400 requests for information on homeschooling—up from a typical five to ten such inquiries. While the pandemic was still raging, clearly many families were making the decision to keep their children safe while also ensuring learning continued in an engaging environment. Unfortunately, so many school systems were forced to go entirely remote, meaning children were glued to their computer screens for up to eight hours a day. For younger children and those with special needs, the monotony is stressful and impedes learning. Even older children can find staring at a screen dull. Whether these numbers hold in a post-Covid world remains to be seen, but I suspect that this exodus could be permanent if families invest the kind of time and preparation necessary for such a program to succeed.

Though I didn't quite realize it at the time, our homeschooling experience would prove mighty beneficial when it came time to retool Divergence towards a totally remote program during the depths of the pandemic.

In retrospect, everything lined up harmoniously for my success. I believe this is because I chose to live in the moment and worked as hard as I could.

If You Don't Ask, You Don't Get

Soon, I applied for Microsoft's Support Engagement Manager position (SEM) at the Desert Mountain District, which included Colorado, Utah, Arizona, New Mexico, Wyoming, and Southern Nevada. (A year later, this position would be rebranded to Support Practice Manager.) I oversaw fifteen technical account managers and in short order found myself preparing for a thorough supervisory review. Wendy G., Vice President of Premier Support, was flying in from Texas to take inventory. My boss, Steve K., (who also reported to Wendy) asked me if I could give her a tour of my Denver customers and introduce her to my team.

As usual, my staff operated at optimal performance. During our one-on-one, Wendy inquired:

"Where do you want to be in five years?"

I responded with something entirely generic:

"I would like to be managing software development issues and related organizations."

"I have an opportunity for you," Wendy said without hesitating. "I want you to interview for another group that operates under my leadership, but it needs a manager. The position has been vacant for three months, and I want you to consider taking on the job."

I immediately started ruminating on all the ways in which I was not enough for the position. I did not take an honest account of my abilities or what I wanted at the time. I thought about the proposition for the rest of the day, then politely declined.

Afterwards, Wendy approached Steve, who later told me about their conversation.

"I don't know what you're building here, but your managers don't know how to take a risk," Wendy had told Steve. "Sravan did not know how to handle something I offered him—something more meaningful, something better than where he is in his career. He does not know how to leap," she said.

Steve probed me for information.

"Did you tell her why this is too risky for you?" he asked.

I paused at the question, surprised by my own lack of communication.

Why hadn't I? I thought.

"You have to pick up the phone and tell her what it's going to take for you to consider the position. Set the parameters. It's in your best interest. If someone taps you on your shoulder and says you are ready for the next move, don't think twice. These things don't happen every day. She's chosen you. You're ready. You've got to communicate what you need and how she can help."

I called Wendy.

"I gave you incomplete information," I said, and I presented the risks that I saw. "My research indicates that you've had six leaders come and go. I do not see how long I'm going to be in the game; if I'm only going to be a temporary leader, it makes no sense for me to pursue this, especially since this position would require a move to Texas."

Wendy assured me that as long as she was the VP of Premier

Support for developers, I would not lose my role. I chose to interview. One of her primary concerns, given my initial behavior, was that I would be fickle. I was interviewed by a fleet of leaders: Peggy T., Brian M., Steve K., and Wendy. I assuaged the team's fears by explaining my intentionality when it comes to navigating risk. Overall, the interview went well, and Wendy hired me as an individual contributor for driving developers' support organization.

I found the transition jarring. I was under the impression I would be given a team. It did not sit well with me that my work would be so similar to my previous position, and that I would be a one man show. I did not want to regress professionally. I felt conflicted, so I reached out to Wendy who provided direction and wisdom that ultimately confirmed my decision:

Management control is not the same thing as leadership. If a person wants to be a leader—they should start by leading. Others will follow. Leaders do not need a team because they see the vision and inherently pull the collective along with them.

And so, I put my reservations aside and I led.

Much of my work had to do with appealing to others. It took a great deal of convincing to get people to adopt my vision, but it paid off. In 2010, we were a $22 million business; by 2012, we were a $44 million business. This increase was largely owed to my instincts and negotiation skills. Our team thrived. Over time, I was able to convince upper management to place more teams under my supervision.

One of the more valuable lessons I learned throughout this

period was how to negotiate. My great mentor Gary R. challenged me to show up every day and give it my best. That I not leave my value on the table. *Show up and share it all. Because if you never show up and never share—you deserve what you get.* He broke it down like this: if a professional is worth $1,000,000 and they only ask for $100,000, the client will meet the minimum every time. That means $900,000 of worth is lying unclaimed on the table. By default, this type of scenario can only yield resentment. This advice would prove essential to my engagements with my clients at Microsoft and to my move into the world of tech startups.

My method was simple: we focused on quality above all else. We gave our time and attention to the solutions that needed the most support, and optimized them to ensure customer satisfaction. This changed how our clients talked about technology. Admittedly, the work was demanding but yielded great results. In turn, I earned the respect of my colleagues.

Change is constant in the business world. After about four years, Wendy was moving on, but she left with parting words of wisdom:

"We know you can build anything. You can take nothing and make something out of it. You are that kind of leader—with clear vision and a sober mind. You can do wonderful stuff. You're a creator of teams and drive growth. We would like to see your leadership thrive." Though Wendy was leaving, I knew I would have opportunities to continue to grow at Microsoft.

Growth in any organization is always good news—even if it indicates risk and turbulence. Essentially, it creates an atmosphere of: *you're up or you're out.* I was now being ushered into a position of greater management. Wendy had primed me for my current endeavors, and I was more than capable of taking on the responsibilities of my predecessors.

I served as the Director of Strategy Innovation until 2014, when I was laid off. I had zero premonition about this. There was no contention, no fallout, no warning sign. In fact, I had come to believe I was beyond having a shelf life. In many ways I had started taking my career for granted. I was forced to recognize one of the most valuable but difficult lessons I have learned thus far: *everyone is replaceable.* In an instant, everything I had built diminished. To my benefit, Microsoft gave me a tremendous severance package. My years at Microsoft equipped me with the skill set I needed to be successful in business. I took the departure as a send-off and heeded my calling—I returned to the drawing board to drum up the next big adventure.

CHAPTER THREE

Crisis Breeds Opportunity

Most people live, whether physically, intellectually, or morally, in a very restricted circle of their potential being. They make use of a very small portion of their possible consciousness, and of their soul's resources in general, much like a man who, out of his whole bodily organism, should get into a habit of using and moving only his little finger. Great emergencies and crises show us how much greater our vital resources are than we had supposed.

William James to Wincenty Lutoslawski [May 6, 1916]

Truth is known when all is seen.

The Upanishads, philosophical Hindu scriptures [6th century BCE]

Only the paranoid survive.

Andrew Grove, CEO, Intel Corp.

Mayank's second surgery in the spring of 2014 coincided with my departure from Microsoft. When we scheduled this additional procedure, my family and I had no idea our lives would be in freefall. Mayank's first cardiologist had been clear with us early on that a second surgery would be necessary. Had I been a young, single entrepreneur, it might have been exhilarating to face the professional abyss. But the daunting reality of seeing my eldest require a second heart surgery was a gut punch. Mayank needed a mitral valve replacement, as his current one was simply not keeping pace with his growing body—no surprise there for a young man of sixteen. The reality of chronic heart conditions is that they require continual maintenance. Though Sangeeta and I knew he would be due at some point for the next procedure, it never got easier knowing he might be in pain or somehow unable to thrive.

We had been prepared for this moment for a few years, though we had only been in Texas since 2011 and hadn't yet developed a long-term relationship with Mayank's new cardiologist. We were nervous enough with the prospect of undertaking a second surgery that Sangeeta emailed Mayank's first cardiologist back in Denver for a second opinion, who concurred that it was time to replace the valve. During one of the early visits to the Texas cardiologist, Mayank was asked if he'd rather step out of the room while Sangeeta and he discussed the forthcoming surgery.

"Mayank, are you sure you want to hear this?" the doctor asked.

"Yes. My parents have never hidden this from me, so there's no point in starting now."

"That's good," replied the doctor. "As you grow, you'll become responsible for taking your medication and staying on top of your treatments, so it's important to start being part of the conversation now."

I was so proud of my son for taking that initiative—Sangeeta was a nervous wreck, but Mayank's proud composure and acceptance fueled us with strength and fortitude. Imagine that.

In the interim, Mayank's scholastic success proved, thankfully, to be the least of our worries: there was no way he could fall behind on his studies when his teacher also happened to be his mother. By the time of Mayank's second surgery, the world of alternative education had ascended to heights perhaps otherwise unimaginable without the assistance of new and emerging technologies. In particular, the tactical deployment of game-based and game-inspired virtual environments specifically targeting school-age children made tremendous gains in a scant six-year window; a 2015 survey conducted by the nonprofit group Speak Up polled 500,000 learners, educators, and parents to gather information regarding their digital consumption, and the intersection of tech and education appeared to have reached an inflexion point by that year. Speak Up found that in 2010, a scant 23 percent of teachers reported using digital games as part of their instruction. That number jumped to 48 percent by 2015. The incorporation of online videos into curricula by teachers leapt from 47 percent to 68 percent over the same period.[1]

Watching videos, learning to code, interacting via social networks—all this was very much on the rise in 2014, with many mainstream think tank wonks and education policy experts finally starting to pay greater attention to the growing impact of digital learning. For my family, incorporating technology and digital methods into education had always been par for the course, even at a time when most institutions would have considered heavy reliance on digital tools to be more of a fringy crutch than beneficial academic enrichment.

As may be imagined, game-based learning tools were hugely important in sustaining the interest of our two homeschooled children. The concept of "gamification" is so much more sophisticated than merely setting a child in front of a screen and letting them play Roblox until their eyes bleed. Rather, gamification as it pertains to academics is the judicious application of game-design components, which can include immediate reward systems, personalized feedback, interactive hint structures, and even controlled content reveals in situations that are not, under normal circumstances, gaming venues.[2] Thoughtful incorporation of these features encourages students to persist, to problem-solve, and to remain engaged over the course of study.

Certainly, plenty of counterarguments exist—namely, that gamification encourages the misuse of digital technology, especially when that technology is placed in the hands of children whose abilities to employ sound judgment and thinking critically are still very much under development. A 2018 study conducted by researchers from Rutgers University found that students perform worse on tests when allowed access to devices like phones and tablets during class.[3] This study was one of the first to examine whether technological distractions would lay waste to the notion that students could multi-task. Spoiler: they can't, but that does not mean that devices should be summarily banned from the ivy-covered gates of academia. Digital learning is here to stay, especially in the wake of the coronavirus pandemic of 2020. The question is how to manage, teach, and interact in meaningful and productive ways. (Sounds like this should have a chapter entirely devoted to it, right? Don't worry, I've got that covered. See Chapter Five for more.)

Abundant Information but Scarce Attention

During and after Mayank's surgery, Sangeeta and I took comfort in the technological powerhouse that is the American medical system, though it certainly helped that we had plenty of doctors and nurses in the family with whom we could discuss the myriad treatments and protocols Mayank was facing. Though there is plenty that needs fixing in the current health care system—Covid-19 has made that clear as a bell—there is still much that it does incredibly well. Mayank was lucky to have a great team at his side. His nurses comforted our family with stories of athletes who persevered and thrived after receiving mitral valve implants. Though there were new treatments in the field of heart surgery, Mayank's situation was such that he required an invasive, open-heart procedure.

During the early, rocky post-op days when Mayank's condition was very much touch-and-go, I sat by his bedside, thinking only of the task in front of me—seeing my son through this process and getting him home. At no time did I even consider what had happened to me professionally. There is no such thing as routine surgery, and that's especially true with open-heart procedures. My only focus was to take care of my son. Days turned into weeks, which turned into a full month in the hospital. Sangeeta and I did nothing but take care of our son. That is what families do in crisis: give total, undivided attention to the person in front of you in need of care. Thankfully, during and after the second surgery, we had unfailing support from friends and family who flew in to help steer the ship at home while Mayank was in the hospital. Even when doctors say, "it's a routine surgery," any parent will tell you that's simply not how it feels. Sometimes, it's the little things that make all the difference: I still recall how our neighbor and her daughter baked brownies and brought them to Mayank. It's a small gesture, but for anyone, some semblance of normalcy is worth its weight in gold.

After about a month in recovery, Mayank turned a corner for the better. The doctors took the feeding tubes out and he began to eat on his own. One day he looked in the mirror and decided he could use a shave, so I picked up a razor and shaving cream and turned the room into a makeshift barbershop. This seemingly insignificant act of facial hair removal was, in fact, cathartic—a signal that Mayank felt strong enough to participate in daily rituals again. And after thirty days of sitting by Mayank's side, I began to actively consider the world of technology all around me. There were x-ray machines enabled with wireless technology wheeled right into the room so that Mayank wouldn't have to make a risky move down to the radiology department. The doctors could simultaneously monitor his brain function and oxygen flow with the touch of a button, and I started thinking about how the great proliferation of digital technology was touching every facet of modern life.

As Mayank's health continued to improve, I finally began to feel some sense of ease and my mind began to explore technology topics again. In particular, I started examining other ways operating rooms were filling up with new technology. For example, by the time Mayank went under the knife for a second time in 2014, telesurgery was already thirteen years old. The first transatlantic virtual surgery had been conducted in September 2001—barely two weeks after the terror attacks that leveled the World Trade Center—when New York surgeons successfully performed gallbladder surgery on a patient in Strasbourg, France.[4] And by that point, robotic surgery was already commonplace in approximately 100 hospitals worldwide.

Though Mayank was unable to benefit from it, robotic mitral surgery was first performed by French doctor Alain Carpentier in 1998 when he used a protype of the now-trademarked da Vinci surgical system, a computer-assisted program designed specifically for heart surgery and now employed in operating rooms across the globe.[5] Over the past twenty years, more than six million robotic-assisted surgeries and procedures have been performed, ranging from cardiac and colorectal to thoracic and general surgeries. Da Vinci robots have proven especially effective at obviating the need for certain types of open-heart surgery. Previously, surgeons had to carve through the breastbone and open the chest to operate on the heart, as was the situation with Mayank. Now, robot-assisted surgery has become routine for procedures such as mitral valve repair. Some surgeries can even be conducted with a catheter inserted through a small incision in the groin that is then threaded towards the heart using the body's vascular system. Fewer complications arise from robotic-assisted surgery, too. Perhaps such an option will be a viable option for someone like my son who may not need to have his chest opened for such a procedure.

Post-surgery, we were surrounded by a hope-bearing staff eager to see Mayank through recovery, however, we were hardly in the clear. One of Mayank's lungs collapsed after the operation, necessitating a three-week hospital stay. In this situation, the newish breathing apparatus wasn't helping Mayank get enough air into his lungs. Rather than try another new machine, the on-call doctor decided to haul out an old device that had been retired years prior. Not that it wasn't serviceable, but the going thought was that newer was always better. The older machine had the type of force necessary to get Mayank's lungs to open but wouldn't put him in further peril.

The only problem was that most of the current hospital staff had no idea how to operate this piece of equipment. Luckily, our doctor had been on staff for decades and witnessed plenty of technology cast aside, only to be dusted off in times of perceived crisis. He trucked out the machine and tested it on himself before signaling to his team that it was safe to use on Mayank. One of the nurses had worked with this machine and became Mayank's guardian angel, tinkering with it to ensure that his breathing was regular. She even coordinated the order of a new bed for Mayank with a better angle that would allow him to breathe fully and unencumbered.

For the first two weeks, this nurse was indispensable. It was clear to me then as now that Mayank wouldn't have recovered as rapidly as he did without her presence. The doctors are indispensable, but it's the support staff—the nurses, the administrative assistants, the clinical coordinators—who do the grunt work, who are there when you're at your worst and lift you up.

Humans living in the twenty-first century have nearly unfettered access to an abundance of information, but attention to that information is scarce. My family's experience with the healthcare system inspired us to become informed participants rather than passive consumers. We read the fine print on *everything* and presented professionals with facts we discovered; in short, refusing to be passed off in the cyclical process of referrals. Our arduous journey led me to conclude that *it's not about the resources that we have, it's about how we use them.*

At the same time, I began to consider the functions of our gadgets and their shelf-lives. We tend to misuse or underuse technology. Televisions, for example, were first envisioned as vessels for educating a wide audience; only a few channels remain dedicated to that lofty goal today. Almost invariably, the optimal functions of machines become secondary to their adapted purposes. For example, the primary function of a cell phone prior to this millennium was to make phone calls. While some early models had access to the internet, we were more likely to use our devices for direct contact, occasional text messages, and a round or two of Snake to kill time. Over time, phone calls became the exception, and these pocket-sized computers became capable of handling everything from banking to teleconferencing with colleagues. We went from racking up huge phone bills with unique ringtone purchases, to keeping them on silent altogether. No one wants to be that guy in the checkout line with his phone loudly exposing his terrible taste in music. Phone calls are no longer the primary function of cellular devices.

A recent study revealed that the average American spends more than eleven hours per day looking at screens, and around twenty percent of that time is given to the consumption of social media.[6] Unless we are going to qualify metabolizing information on our peers' personal lives as research, it is safe to assume that we employ these gadgets at their minimum abilities rather than optimizing them to their greatest potential.

My layoff from Microsoft, paired with months observing machines in the hospital, led me to ponder the myriad ways I could get the most out of our devices. Sangeeta and I had already incorporated the use of computers into our homeschooling methods. I was a tech guy, so of course, my children were going to be tech savvy, but what about other Americans? Or those who needed to switch careers because theirs was being replaced or updated by technology? How about those who found themselves adrift on the sea of online course offerings? These thoughts began to percolate in my mind. Virtual classes were proving to be the wave of the future, not just for our kids, but for the greater population. As colleges accommodated new models for learning, I took interest in the arguments of naysayers. As a species, humans are judgmental, and, unfortunately, most skeptics are misinformed. Sangeeta and I were practiced at engaging antagonists, especially regarding education modalities.

We found ourselves constantly defending our choice to homeschool due to outdated stereotypes. Some of the most brilliant artists, writers, athletes, and thriving business professionals were homeschooled. Condoleezza Rice, Serena and Venus Williams, George Washington, Thomas Edison, and yes, even Justin Bieber were all taught at home. Remember, I am a product of a non-traditional education, so it's fair to say that I practice what I preach, and it is inaccurate to assume those who are not educated in a conventional setting are socially inept, uncultured, or undereducated. When provided effectively, homeschooling and alternative education modes can yield *greater* opportunity and better results than well-worn traditional pathways.

It was this consideration, paired with my evolving relationship with technology, that inspired my next big idea. I began brainstorming ways to revolutionize the education system. I had yet to hear of a satisfying online learning experience. I knew there was a growing market for virtual solutions, and I had the skill set to lay the foundation. As usual, I brought Sangeeta to the drawing board, and she was thrilled at the concept.

In the midst of chaos, we began to dream.

Nothing Happens Overnight

Part of contributing to a burgeoning industry is learning to balance the value and possibility of implementing new ideas. I have grown fond of a concept popular among tech giants culled from the mind of futurist Roy Amara (1925-2007), and I think it distills what I'm trying to say here: *never overestimate the effect of technology in the short run while underestimating technology in the long run.* The evolution of any technology never happens overnight. It took up to five years of investing and improvements before cell phones became a huge component of our lives. Now, we cannot live without them. This has presented some unprecedented challenges. Stimulation overload has resulted in attention scarcity. Too much information drives inattentiveness—which, by default, creates new opportunities for technology to later solve.

People in my line of work love solving problems. (If they don't, I'm pretty sure they're in the *wrong* line of work.) Perhaps the most challenging element of solving a problem—sometimes even more difficult than the execution of the solution—is coming up with the idea in the first place. Luckily, the tech world is awash in new ideas. I'd venture to say that idea overload is commonplace in the tech world. Teams come in with revolutionary nuggets sparked by something they heard, read, or saw. Everyone is always pitching—*hey! We should do this, too!* While this makes environments like Microsoft an oversaturated landscape of intellectual curiosity, it is also what makes them a success. Thriving businesses know how to assess the value of an idea in the moment and how to maximize its potential and sustainability for the future.

Those who thrive in the technology sector are always looking at ways to bolster revenue, build sustainable partnerships, and generate market appeal. Something I have learned to ask myself and my team continually is: *What is the next step?*

Taking an idea to the next level is about committing to one expansive concept and not getting sidetracked by endless distractions. I try to approach all things in life from a streamlined perspective. Consistency is key, but willingness to pivot is a critical skill. And, above all, it is imperative to stay out of the weeds.

Easier said than done, but not impossible. Not by a long shot.

I seared these principles into my mind while venturing into the professional unknown. After extensive research on education modules, I decided that I wanted to build a learning academy. My vision was to create a modernized learning environment dedicated to versatility and technology optimization. My goal was to help students narrow their trajectory towards a practical outcome by offering them something few other schools do: the very real possibility of a job at the end of it all.

Most learning institutions provide four-year plans packed with expensive and oftentimes unnecessary classes. My experience with the world's leading professionals at Microsoft taught me it's far more valuable to acquire a specific skill set than it is to have a general degree. Information is the most powerful tool when utilized correctly—my vision was to teach learners how to harness the most useful information to further their professional plans.

To appeal to two generations of learners, those steeped in technology—the so-called digital natives, as well as those with no real background in the field—it was imperative to hold their attention and present them with a correlating, near-term benefit—a real world application of gamification, in essence. This would be difficult due to existing attention scarcity, since competing colleges targeted recruits with information overload.

I wanted to provide the opposite experience.

By creating an institution that streamlined choices as opposed to amplifying endless possibilities, I knew I could improve the experience of the consumer. The modern learner knows how to use tools to communicate quickly, but determining educational benefits can be challenging, especially when alternate forms of education are deemed suspect. I knew once I could create marketable learning solutions, I could encourage my learners to establish a tribe.

Establishing a tribe is imperative for nearly every element of a business, and I believe the same goes for an education company. No entrepreneur thrives when going at it alone. Due to the apprehensions of society at large, those who focus on unconventional learning models will always experience some form of pushback. Change is good, but change is also often unwelcome and hard to initiate. Perseverance is key. Discovering and facilitating a tribe excites the market about the product. My responsibility was to create a system that was affordable and beneficial to its consumers. Determining the profile of my academy's ideal student helped me predict areas of need and determine my methods for success.

One surprising statistic I encountered while researching online education is that 90 percent of students abandon coursework within a week of starting.[7] Yet, upon further reflection, this statistic makes total sense: most online coursework is tedious and fueled by the personal goals of financial advisors who specialize in doling out information for unreasonable course requirements while sneaking in hidden fees. It's no wonder that the vast majority of would-be learners feel entirely deflated. Why pursue a formal education at all? If a person wants to learn a skill or pick up new business hacks, there's always YouTube. And YouTube offers some amazing content, but at the end of the day, scrolling through video feeds is ad hoc and unfocused. There's no accountability—who cares if you stop for a week or two? No one's there to encourage you to keep going or to talk you through a difficult concept. (There's a reason why it's not called WeTube—watching videos on a portable device is an inherently solitary affair.) There seemed to be no online platform that focused on the *we*. People do not thrive in isolation.

One of the risks I anticipated while establishing a system that prioritized maximal information over a minimal timeframe was that learners would not absorb the materials. As I also discovered, learners more often than not have little opportunity to build a relationship with their online professors. This lack of support, paired with information overload, can create a sense of isolation. Learning and anxiety cannot co-exist in the same space. This inspired the profile of the ideal instructor. I knew employing educators that *only* directed online classes would run counter to my overall mission. Therefore, I decided it would be best to offer an option that accommodated all learning styles. That was the value prop: learners could gain specific skills, a portfolio, and a supportive community in a matter of ten weeks through a carefully targeted combination of in-person and online instruction.

No one thrives when distracted. I knew I had to foster a culture dedicated to harnessing focused intentions. The reality was that some *would* struggle with taking on 400 hours of coursework in less than three months. Many of our learners would hail from non-traditional pathways: adult learners, career switchers, learners holding down day jobs, and others. For those learners, it was imperative to offer them assistance. To that end, I mapped out support systems tailored specifically to these learning cohorts, including late night coaching options, group study sessions, learning accommodations, and one-to-one counseling.

My primary goal was to establish a strong sense of values early on and only hire the best. That meant looking for people who believed in the mission. Technology is teachable. Anyone can learn it. I wanted to recruit people who wanted to put in the hard work. Ultimately, we built candidate profiles of a learner and instructor excited by the opportunity to overcome obstacles. Throughout my years of working with big tech clients, I had learned a lot about assessing the character of others. Sometimes, I missed the mark. But most of the time my intuition—based on prior experience and accumulated knowledge—proved to be on point. I knew my business had to be built on good instinct. It was important to me to draw investors who shared and challenged my philosophies so that I would be forced to prove their value in both word and deed.

I set out to find talent with the ability to deliver. My hope was to create a regenerative environment where I would eventually hire my own graduates to contribute to the culture. Cultivating a community of leaders was one of my highest priorities. People learn by teaching. The notion of keeping learners on staff appealed to me because they would be an active demonstration of the product, and a constant example of learners devoted to continuing their education. I wanted the school to be a story in and of itself of diversity, inclusion, investment, and loyalty.

My journey proves that, despite fallow seasons, with constant tending and attention, *there will be growth.* Additionally, it is imperative that all growth happens at a reasonable pace. If expansion happens too quickly the business loses the opportunity to properly instill cornerstone philosophies and facilitate outstanding leadership. Nothing worth having is built in a day.

Do it boldly, do it correctly, and do it with value and purpose.

What's in a Name

I often say my children are the original founders of my academy. Their pictures are up on the wall in the main hallway. My family and I have always pursued opportunity as a collective endeavor. When considering a name for the institution, I invited their collaboration. At the time, Trisha was thirteen and a ravenous reader and prolific writer. In 2011, the book *Divergent* by Veronica Roth became a *New York Times* bestseller. By 2014, the sci-fi dystopian trilogy had been made into the first of three movies starring Shailene Woodley. Empowered by the central themes of self-discovery and independence in the face of seemingly insurmountable challenges espoused throughout the movie, Trisha's unbridled enthusiasm for the movie intrigued me to the point where I began seriously considering the meaning of the word "divergent" beyond its immediate usage. Was there anything more dissimilar than the dream I was trying to build with my school? Upon closer examination, I realized that divergent could be a synonym for independent, and that's how I viewed my school. Our mission capitalized on transcendence. It was about boldness, versatility, and the tenacity to revolutionize education and leadership. While Mayank's critical period in the hospital inspired the vision of Divergence Academy, Trisha's creativity inspired its name.

The origins of Divergence were and always have been a family affair. From setting the aesthetic to considering the future of the school from a learner's perspective, my family has had a say in what goes where. That said, Divergence is technically not a family business—I didn't inherit the business from my parents, nor do I expect my children to continue the tradition (though it wouldn't upset me if they did!)—but I have never thrived in business without my family offering advice and guidance along the way.

I have often wondered if trials and miracles exist on some kind of continuum. It is as if there is a specific space, between utter chaos and plain old luck, where dreams are born. Our dream was born in a state of freefall. Our year of chaos reinforced the concept of tenacity and perseverance for everyone in my family, and a new business idea was born, too. Despite illness, professional failure, financial setbacks, and moments of sheer panic, we kept imagining. We kept moving forward. Remember, when faced with chaos, try all the doors. One will be the entrance to your next opportunity.

CHAPTER FOUR

Curation Is Greater than Creation: Bridging the Gap

Society can only be understood through a study of the messages and the communication facilities which belong to it; and that in the future development of these messages and communication facilities, messages between man and machines, between machines and man, and between machine and machine, are destined to play an ever increasing part.

Norbert Wiener, The Human Use of Human Beings [1950]

After more than a century of electric technology, we have extended our central nervous system itself in a global embrace, abolishing both space and time as far as our planet is concerned. Rapidly, we approach the final phase of the extensions of man—the technological simulation of consciousness, when the creative process of knowing will be collectively and corporately extended to the whole of human society, much as we have already extended our senses and our nerves by the various media.

Marshal McLuhan, Understanding Media [1964]

Norbert Wiener was a Hungarian-born mathematician, electrical engineer, and communications specialist whose exploration of human-machine interaction in his 1948 volume *Cybernetics* can credibly be considered one of the earliest technical treatises on the coexistence of man and machine. Despite what he says were his best efforts, Wiener couldn't readily find a term to classify this exciting development in the world of technological automation, so he created his own: derived from the Greek work for "steersman," and "governor," *kubernētēs*—anglicized to "cybernetics"—seemed to capture the concept of this new field of thought. Even in the 1950s, Wiener was already presaging the coming gap between those who understood how to communicate with machines and those who did not:

> It is my thesis that the physical functioning of the living individual and the operation of some of the newer communication machines are precisely parallel in their analogous attempts to control entropy through feedback. Both of them have sensory receptors as one stage in their cycle of operation; that is, in both of them there exists a special apparatus for collecting information from the outer world at low energy levels, and for making it available in the operation of the individual or of the machine. In both cases these external messages are not taken neat, but through the internal transforming powers of the apparatus, whether it be alive or dead. The information is then turned into a new form available for the further stages of performance.[1]

In lay terms: Wiener is looking at the rise of the machines and saying that these creations of our own design are not here to destroy us, as many fear; instead, there are beneficial and practical applications of learning to communicate with machines so long as we are willing to make the effort. I will take it a step further and assert that, while there are risks inherent in delegating more of our lives to artificial intelligence, harnessed appropriately this brave new partnership offers limitless potential to pursue our most fulfilling and rewarding lives while also solving many of the world's great problems. Part of that "contract" is our willingness to understand and control this technology, not to be passive participants and idle consumers but leaders capable of guiding this science to where we need it and adapting our own capabilities as the technology advances. That, dear readers, requires constant upskilling and education.

So, time to enroll in a traditional four-year college program, right? Hold on to your wallets. Unfortunately, most traditional colleges are leaving learners woefully unprepared for the future that is very much already upon us. This is not new, but most educators have been willing to turn a blind eye to this growing dilemma for too long. The recent events of 2020 have laid bare the truth that we must reskill or be left behind in the inexorable march towards a more digitized and automated future.

And yes, though most of us would probably rather see the year 2020 confined to the dustbin of history, we cannot allow recent events to go by without learning something from them. We faced a global pandemic, which, at the time of writing, shows no signs of abating and has killed an unfathomable 580,000-plus people in America alone; an economic downturn disproportionately impacting low-income groups and people of color but that is also starting to attack more white-collar, middle class workers; and a civil reckoning the likes of which haven't been seen in the United States in fifty years. Add to that the growing chaos wreaked by human-induced climate change and the unrelenting march of technology, and no one would blame you if you'd prefer to stick your head in the sand and give up.

But we're not going to do that. Hear me out.

I think that despite these grave challenges we have a tremendous opportunity to harness our cumulative intellect and talent to face these issues straight on by providing tangible solutions that foster long-term change rather than mere palliative care. Scientists created a vaccine for Covid-19 in record time, and even in the dark days of the pandemic, fewer people died of Covid-19 overall as doctors gained more experience treating patients.[2] When president Donald J. Trump fell ill with Covid-19, his medical team got him on then-experimental antibody regimens which likely helped him to a speedy recovery. The development of successful vaccines in less than a year was unprecedented in its pace and could not have happened using old technologies.

Civil unrest will lead to constructive dialogue and positive change. Demands for visibility and parity are being heard, and steps are being taken to achieve those goals. Slowly, the economy will start to bounce back as well. It is on this last point that I would like to elaborate further. Though the economy will rebound eventually, many parts of the economy will reemerge bearing little resemblance to how they looked prior to the pandemic. Which brings us back to the education sector. Covid forced change and drove tech advances that were ten years down the road, setting them in motion now. Some of us adapted better than others, and I believe that this is a test run for further tech disruption looming on the horizon. We need to be prepared or prepare to be left behind, jobless and unskilled.

Pre-pandemic, underprivileged and underserved communities faced teacher shortages, funding cuts, and a lack of enrichment opportunities. Those disparities grew more pronounced during the crisis. Some school districts were prepared for disasters with backup plans ready to go; consider school systems in the Northeast, for example, where snow can regularly hinder classroom instruction. Many of these districts had already moved to online learning as an auxiliary mode of education and endured less disruption when stay at home orders were invoked. This was the case only in those districts that had more money to play with; those serving disadvantaged communities could not pivot as easily.[3] Regardless, new research is revealing that the majority of students in the United States are months behind where they should be in their scholastic journeys, regardless of how well their schools weathered the darkest days of the pandemic.[4]

Many school districts cannot afford books, let alone technology. Meaningless paper pushing does not equip students for success and ultimately deteriorates learner self-esteem. Why try when there's no light at the end of the tunnel? Even the most prepared school districts were financially crippled by the overwhelming need for laptops and corresponding software. Technology that was considered a luxury became critical. In moderate to low-income districts, parents were asked to contribute their personal resources to furnish children's at-home workspaces. With little instruction and zero additional reward, learners became exhausted as circumstances worsened.

Though technological shifts have been transforming the way students learn for decades, the pandemic unleashed a seismic shift from in-person to virtual and flexible offerings, which we'll discuss in greater detail shortly. Now that the divide has been made even wider, educators face another dilemma—namely, that accepting the old way of teaching is no longer a viable model. The rate of technological progress is rendering some coursework obsolete even before graduates have the chance to test those skills out in the marketplace. As early as middle school, math students are still being taught to use calculators that have no practical real-world application; these children should really be learning how to use Microsoft Excel. It is incredibly unfair for the traditional academic system to insist that students spend ten or more years of their lives plodding through curricula that will undoubtedly be irrelevant and obsolete once those students enter the workforce. Then what, send the students back to school for further training? Sure, picking up a course here and there may be no big deal, but leaving an entire generation unequipped to meet the forthcoming demands of a tech-based ecosystem puts American workers at a serious disadvantage. The entire curriculum needs to be revamped and nimble enough to evolve as technology does.

Elite universities such as MIT, the California Institute of Technology (Caltech), and Harvard have the resources and the drive to educate using next-generation technology, support cutting-edge research initiatives, and serve as innovative incubators for new ideas. But not everyone has the standardized test scores or funds to get into these schools, and where does that leave most learners? Trickle-down academics will not suffice. Being adequately skilled to meet the needs of a digital economy should not be something reserved for geniuses and those with fat bank accounts. The new economy will require that most of its participants be capable of maneuvering from one skill set to another. Though I'm confident in Caltech's ability to teach skills for future needs, how can the majority of American universities prepare learners for technology that may not yet exist? Bridging the gap between what schools offer and what learners need is far more time-consuming than throwing around empty phrases like "optimizing user interfaces." Once again, the looming issue for most schools is a total curriculum overhaul. Clearly, that is not going to happen overnight, so what can learners do in the meantime? A willingness to diverge from the so-called "traditional academic path" may be a good place to start. I see my school as a bridge that straddles the divide—a vocational school for the digital age.

Nothing Happens in a Vacuum

Divergence did not experience overnight success: in fact, October 2019 was the first time we had fifteen students in one classroom. Until that point, our maximum class size had hovered between eight and eleven. I knew I wanted to innovate through education, and soon came to the conclusion that while I was building my own company, I'd also have to build my own framework that focused on foresight, innovation, and transformation in the field of technological education.

I started tinkering with the idea of building my school in 2014. First, I needed a home for it. We found a space in downtown Addison called Addison Treehouse, a startup incubator and coworking space akin to WeWork, and this served as a temporary Divergence base of operations.

At the Treehouse, I began hosting three to four monthly discussions primarily to start drumming up interest in Divergence. Since we weren't approved to operate yet, I couldn't advertise, but I could talk about my vision, which I did at every opportunity.

Though my school was still a few months from opening day, I needed to get people interested in signing up once we were in business, which I did by hosting on-campus discussions about trending topics in the field of data technology. One of our most successful such programs was called Hamlet on the Holodeck, a discussion based on the 1997 book by Janet Murray that explored the rise of digital storytelling at the intersection of traditional media and innovation. This conversation examined how Shakespeare's *Hamlet* has managed to captivate audiences for centuries; then we talked about weaving that tale into the world of the internet of things. In other words, we wanted to discuss how we might tell this story in the present era and how technology afforded us an opportunity to alter the story as we saw fit. With video-on-demand, *Hamlet* could be live-streamed anywhere or anytime. If we were feeling particularly saucy, we could change the ending: that is the power of imagination. (But is it still *Hamlet*?) In addition, we parsed the ever-growing influence of the internet and the continued relevance of futurist and *2001: A Space Odyssey* co-author Arthur C. Clarke's three laws of technology, dictums that state:

1. When a distinguished but elderly scientist states that something is possible, he is almost certainly right. When he states that something is impossible, he is very probably wrong.

2. The only way of discovering the limits of the possible is to venture a little way past them into the impossible.

3. Any sufficiently advanced technology is indistinguishable from magic.[5]

We discussed how this new kind of thinking required new modes of leadership, how creativity and innovation should no longer be trendy topics but instead must be integral components of future organizations. With today's capabilities, you can go beyond reading *Hamlet* and actually play the title role. My overall goal with this program was to encourage prospective students to apply for admission to this newly launched vocational tech school.

Another major push came when I participated in the 2015 iteration of Dallas Startup Week. Though the media may make it seem so, startups don't just fall from the sky. They are born when a person or group thinks of something that may solve a problem or create an opportunity for others. Think of Airbnb—it grew out of co-founder and CEO Brian Chesky's simple desire to make extra money by renting out his San Francisco apartment. Today, with the help of venture capital, Airbnb is valued at over $100 billion. Nothing happens in a vacuum: Chesky has startup funder Y Combinator to thank for infusing Airbnb with cash to get off the ground.

I considered my school to be a startup. I wanted to fill the void that was technological education by retooling learners; the future Dallas Startup Week was an appropriate venue to talk it up and to meet amazing fellow entrepreneurs and investors while practicing my elevator pitch, all while generating interest in Divergence.

Finally, on May 17, 2015, after what seemed like eons, Divergence was approved by the state of Texas to operate as a school. Considering that nine months prior I had just been laid off, this might be considered warp speed. For me, those nine months were excruciatingly painful.

Then, students were knocking our door down, right? Not quite. It took four months before we welcomed our first two students, Dominic Yang and Murali Ramamoorthy. These were the first two brave souls to join Divergence. Dominic had just graduated from the University of Texas at Dallas and didn't know what he wanted to do with his degree. He also didn't feel like his undergraduate education had sufficiently prepared him for any kind of serious employment. Both Dominic and Morali were willing to pay the $3,000 tuition for our six-week, 60-hour "short course" intensive program. To accommodate our duo, who each held down jobs Monday through Friday, that first program took place over a series of weekends, with me leading the instruction. By mid-October we had graduated our first cohort. Like many startups, I was a one-man army, and my modest goal for the rest of 2015 was to see Divergence survive another year.

While our inaugural cohort was buckling down, I received a call from Orlando Campos, the director of economic development for the city of Addison. His offices were also at Addison Treehouse, the same building as our first headquarters for Divergence Academy. In addition to sharing coffee breaks when we would discuss our collective efforts to build a school and businesses in Addison, Campos eventually introduced me to representatives at Richland College through one of his connections at the Texas Workforce Commission.

"Sravan, I've just been to an event hosted by the Texas Workforce Commission," Campos said one day. "Turns out that Richland College needs help getting grants to fund their workforce development programs, and I think you would be the right person to help them out." Campos recalled my presentation at Dallas Startup Week where I had talked about my background in business training. I was intrigued, so I met the coordinators at Richland College. They were working on securing a tech grant from the state that would allow them to partner with Dallas-based RealPage, a global provider of software and data analytics to the real estate industry. RealPage was willing to send their employees to Richland for a short training so that students could learn a new skill. Much of Richland's educational focus was on manufacturing, so pivoting to IT training was out of their comfort zone. The school's administrators recognized that IT was a necessary skill for their students. This grant would help them meet the demand.

It took an entire year to get approval, but by October 2016, Richland College had secured a $1.2 million grant from the Texas Workforce Commission Skills Development Fund.[6]

Now, you're wondering how this benefitted me. In fact, on the surface it sounds like Richland's pivot to IT might make it a competitor to Divergence. For starters, I made excellent connections at the Texas Workforce Commission that I didn't have before—I could see how such a partnership would entice cash-strapped students interested in retooling. And I finally saw firsthand what I had long known to be true: that there was a massive unmet need for schools to provide customized training on cloud software, project management, and IT. Divergence differed from the Richland program because we offered far more than generic IT programming. But I believed—and still do—that we could function in tandem by supporting learners at various stages and needs.

Divergence continued to grow. Slowly, we began recruiting

students from various local companies where employees needed to upskill to remain relevant and secure promotions. However, by this time our program had expanded, and the cost went up accordingly. There is no getting around the fact that $13,000 for a twelve-week, 480-hour course requires a major commitment. And Divergence was still a relative unknown—understandably, learners were apprehensive, and many needed financial assistance. Our real breakthrough came when Beth L., my first employee and de facto program director, came upon a new method to attract students and help Divergence gain legitimacy in academic circles.

"There is so much more opportunity if we can focus on professionals in transition—people who've recently become unemployed," Beth explained. "We need to explore the Workforce Innovation and Opportunity Act. It's a funding program that helps Americans facing barriers to employment find high-quality jobs. Part of that funding comes from the U.S. Departments of Labor and Education." Specifically, Beth learned that people going through career transitions will go to workforce centers certified by WIOA and reskill. Most importantly, WIOA provides financial assistance, but again, only if your school is on the approved list. Of course, we applied.

By May 2017, two years after Divergence had opened its doors, WIOA added us to the list of eligible training provider systems. Here's how it works: Let's say someone is unemployed or looking to change careers, doesn't know where to look for state-funded and approved programs, or needs financial assistance to pursue additional education; he or she will go to the WIOA database and look up relevant programs and apply for financial assistance. This process could easily become overwhelming and Divergence could have gotten lost among the many dozens of offerings. Beth, however, made sure to visit the various workforce centers and talk to prospective learners about the benefits of retooling with an eye towards data science.

Two more students, Jason Besly and Mary Helen Krause, signed up for the twelve-week program.

Two students enrolling every six weeks wasn't going to cut it. I was beginning to think that perhaps Dallas wasn't the right place for a school that focused on data analytics—maybe an IT hub like New York or California would be better. Certainly, it was tempting to think that geography was the problem, but that wasn't the case. I knew that, eventually, emerging IT solutions would be commonplace, and every business would need people capable of manipulating the technology. It was just that the companies based in the Dallas area—PepsiCo, Texas Instruments, and ExxonMobil, among others—were far more focused at the time on streamlining manufacturing and automation rather than on data analytics. How could I convince these companies that my school was offering programs they and their employees needed? How could I make data science make sense to businesspeople for whom the term "IT" belonged in an episode of *Star Trek* and not in their boardrooms. I started to think about the practical uses of data science and landed on cybersecurity. Every company, no matter what they sell, needs cybersecurity and people on their teams to implement it.

Bingo. We revamped our course offerings and updated our profile in the state's education development guide. By April 2018, our cybersecurity program launched, and we were filled. I finally hired instructors to help me out.

When we wanted to scale up even further, we had to figure out what new well of students we could draw from. That's when we realized we should be looking at the U.S. Department of Veterans Affairs, which had recently listed a new program on their website called the Veteran Employment Through Technology Courses (VET TEC) program. Veterans are natural leaders and comfortable working in teams to get the job done. High pressure environments are expected. Veterans have an enviable work ethic and give their all to every task at hand. Further, companies that hire veterans are eligible for the Returning Heroes Tax Credit. If a veteran with a service-related disability is hired, then the company can be eligible for a Wounded Warriors Tax Credit. These tax credits can save employers up to $9,600 on employee salary costs. We started marketing Divergence to veterans and to local employers with these facts in mind.

Veterans should not be overlooked when it comes to recruitment, especially in the tech industry. We set a goal at Divergence Academy to place veterans into high-tech jobs no later than 180 days after taking our course. Many of our graduates ultimately end up working in the fields of cybersecurity or IT infrastructure. And America's veterans are ideally suited to take on this kind of work.

Here are a few of our graduates who have answered the country's call to serve on the battlefields of cybersecurity and intelligence.

Charles Gilpin enlisted in the U.S. Army in 2009 as an IT specialist. From the outset, he was tasked with maintaining and troubleshooting military computer systems, so by the time he came to us in 2019, he had a foundation in computer science. Charles started moving up the ranks, from computer specialist to information technology manager, where he was tasked with leading dozens of other specialists and programmers whose mission was to upgrade hundreds of outdated and obsolete computer systems. Then, in 2019, Charles hit an impasse. He was no longer on active duty and wanted to take on more challenges in the field of data science. So, he decided to pursue an IT certification with a focus on cybersecurity. The program has given Charles the confidence to pursue upper management positions in IT troubleshooting and network security.

"The cybersecurity professional penetration tester course is not easy—you can't expect to just show up and pass," Charles said. "You will put in the work on the nights and weekends to succeed." We invest in our learners, and in turn, their investment in their education pays dividends.

Anthony Hunter is another recent graduate who, like Charles, came to Divergence as a veteran—of the Air Force in this case. After spending eight years managing law enforcement and security operations at Cheyenne Mountain Air Force Station, Anthony was ready for something new. In February 2019, he moved to Texas to serve as the technology specialist for the Canton Independent School District. To continue in his role of accurately troubleshooting technology support requests, Anthony knew he needed more knowledge to fulfill his job to the best of his ability, and he found Divergence. "I wanted to make sure that the program I chose was worth my time and money," he said. "They [Divergence] have some of the best instructors I have ever seen. The instructors have the technical knowledge that is both real and valuable, and they make sure they are teaching to all levels, no matter what your experience." After completing his bootcamp program, Anthony landed a new job as a security analyst at DefendEdge in Chicago, Illinois.

My strategy as a progressive educator has always been to equip my students with a sustainable foundation upon which they can build a life. Digital technology requires fresh skills. But, unlike the world of computer science a generation ago, the skills needed to survive in the workplace today are teachable—and that is the great inflection point at which we find ourselves now. Technology itself is not a job, but it is a *means* to a job. It can move people to new places—new places of employment, for example. But the job itself will evolve more quickly than the work of yore. Meaningful employment in the tech field means arriving with a basic skill set plus an ability to adapt to new technology as it comes down the pike.

At Divergence, my staff and I are committed to teaching veterans—and our other learners—adaptability so that they can provide for themselves in the new tech economy. As Divergence has grown, we consider the needs of learners who might need extra support—including exceptional learners and those with alternate abilities. Unlike legacy education providers, we built our school to thrive with the evolution of technology, not to be bogged down with each new technological innovation. Our axis has always hinged on mobility. I learned early in my career that businesses that do not utilize new tools will atrophy. Anyone can learn technology. The challenge is maintaining an adaptable approach as the need for technology grows and the technology itself evolves.

The last point I'd like to make here is that change is happening faster now than ever before in human history—we've only had a taste of that rapid clip with the coronavirus pandemic, and it's only going to accelerate. Robots are here, yes, and they are taking old jobs once completed by humans, but we needn't fear them. Nor are we becoming cyborgs as Elon Musk opined during a 2017 interview with Maureen Dowd in *Vanity Fair.*[7] I firmly believe that not only will we coexist, we humans will remain in charge.

And moving forward, I want Divergence to focus on training those robots, too. Norman Weiner was right: we need to talk to the machines, but we also need to train them. Follow me to read about building a stronger bridge to the future.

CHAPTER FIVE
A Virus Accelerates Change

You'll see that, since our fate is ruled by chance,
Each man, unknowing, great
Should frame life so that at some future hour
Fact and his dreamings meet.
Victor Hugo, *To His Orphan Grandchildren* [1871]

When the great French poet Victor Hugo wrote this poem, he was drawing from a very personal well of experience: his 44-year-old son, Charles Hugo, had suffered a fatal stroke en route to visit friends in Bordeaux. Charles's wife died shortly thereafter, leaving Victor the guardian of his grandchildren, Georges and Jeanne. At least on the surface, many poems in this collection celebrate life despite the bleakest of circumstances, but there is nothing childish about these musings. Throughout, Hugo deftly finds ways to revisit his preferred themes of equality for all while railing against bigotry and tyranny. In this stanza from *To His Orphan Grandchildren*, Hugo looks to the future, with hope that unlike in the ancient world ruled by aristocrats, modern men and women of all backgrounds will have the opportunity to forge their own destinies as they see fit. We too are masters of our futures and should not forget this as we face what may increasingly feel like a destiny dictated by artificial intelligence and digital technology.

And yet, there's no changing the fact that technology has forever altered how we live our lives, as each innovation has done since early *Homo sapiens* first struck flint to kindling, but that does not mean we must cede control to the unknown. In fact, there is much that we can do to arm ourselves with the knowledge necessary to enjoy a bright and productive future. Much of that preparedness will require a redoubled focus on education, both how it is delivered and what that education entails.

Technological shifts have been transforming the way students learn for decades. The arrival of the novel coronavirus unleashed a seismic shift from in-person to virtual and flexible offerings. I'd like to examine those shifts here by exploring the changes that have taken place at the intersections of education and technology, and how I believe a nuanced and open-minded approach is the best way forward for the majority of Americans seeking better opportunities for themselves and their families.

When stay-at-home orders rolled out in March 2020—specifically in hard-hit places like New York, California, Massachusetts, Michigan, and New Jersey—most people did just that: office workers packed up their stations, gave their desk plants one final soaking, and embarked on what many thought would be a week or two indulging in the work-from-home lifestyle.

Six months later, the results of working from home during the pandemic were in, and the numbers were dramatic. Aside from millions of desiccated Ficus plants trapped in office high-rises, the pandemic led to an American economy that pivoted—in a matter of weeks—from one based on commuting to one that relied on Wi-Fi connectivity. The shift to working from home was, in many ways, historic: a study conducted by Stanford University revealed that fully 42 percent of the entire U.S. labor force shifted to working full-time from their homes, representing more than two-thirds of all economic activity in the United States.[1] Further, as of publication, these workers will likely continue to earn their keep from home until 2022, even though now a vaccine is widely available. Meanwhile, 33 percent of employees reported that they were not working from home through the pandemic—either because they could not perform their job remotely or because they had been laid off. Another 26 percent of American workers were deemed "essential" and had to continue going to their places of employment, often putting themselves and their families in danger of contracting a virus that was still barely understood and with long-term health consequences due to exposure to the virus still undetermined. In addition to front-line healthcare workers, people in positions previously considered "entry-level" became pandemic heroes: grocery clerks, delivery workers, public transportation conductors, slaughterhouse employees, and farmworkers. Many workers in these industries did not have sufficient access to health care or personal protective equipment for themselves. Still others refrained from calling in sick for fear of possibly losing their job. Some even died from contracting the virus because they were working to protect the rest of us.

Now, some politicians are paying it forward for those who stepped up when so many of us could not. In September 2020, six months after the pandemic brought most of American life to a standstill, the state of Michigan announced a new education initiative called the Futures for Frontliners program which offers free community college tuition to essential workers. In this case, the phrase "essential workers" extended beyond doctors and nurses to include those pandemic heroes mentioned above. Those eligible for the program include workers who had to leave their homes to do their jobs while the pandemic raged on. It is the latest state to offer tuition-free community college education for residents, and is believed to be the first to specifically court those who provided frontline services between April and June of 2020—which, in Michigan, numbers around 625,000 residents.

"This initiative is Michigan's way of expressing gratitude to essential workers for protecting public health and keeping our state running. Whether it was stocking shelves, delivering supplies, picking up trash, manufacturing PPE or providing medical care, you were there for us. Now this is your chance to pursue the degree or training you've been dreaming about to help you and your own family succeed," said Governor Gretchen Whitmer.

Funded entirely with a $24 million investment from the

Governor's Emergency Education Relief Fund, the program is a major recognition on the part of a state government that a more educated workforce is essential to growing businesses and helping families navigate what is increasingly becoming an automated, data-driven economy.

This is a huge initiative, but I think we need to examine it critically to see exactly what potential students would be getting out of this program and others like it. An associate degree is a two-year program, and in Michigan's case, eligible students must have no existing debt, and the program is only available to those whose combined household incomes maxes out at $26,000. There are plenty of degrees to choose among, from business management to graphic design and criminal justice. However, only two of the community colleges offer data science and computer science programs. Given the broad reach of this endeavor, will the majority of those 625,000 potential students actually enroll in the program? It's unlikely; financial assistance addresses only one of many barriers to education learners face.

In an interview with National Public Radio, Michigan Department of Labor and Economic Opportunity representative Jeff Donofrio did not believe the program would be as attractive to potential students as it could be. "You know, when you start these types of programs, you're making a lot of assumptions around how many people will be eligible, how many people will want to take you up on the opportunity," Donofrio said. "And I think we're in a period of time with COVID where it's not really that clear how all those assumptions are going to work out. I think it would be a good problem for us to have, though, that too many people sign up." This program was limited in duration as well: since the funding was tied to the federal CARES Act, the application deadline was December 31, 2020.

Were this to be a true attempt to foster systemic academic change, this kind of opportunity would not disappear with the flip of a calendar. Further, it is not clear that the degrees being conferred are indeed those that will result in better-paying jobs. Yes, having a degree beyond a high school diploma is necessary to securing a higher-paying (and probably more secure) job, but I do not think the education system is taking into account the x-factor that is artificial intelligence and the unrelenting march of technology. I fear that these degrees will not be a fail-safe against future job loss.

Additionally, there is no mention of how the academic system will support these learners through their journey. As I mentioned above, financial assistance is only one factor that hinders would-be learners from completing a degree. In a state where an estimated 43 percent of all households—that's 1.66 million homes across Michigan—cannot afford basic necessities like childcare, food, and health care, learners who even demonstrate a passing interest in pursuing this program will need far more assistance beyond having their tuition covered. It is still too early to tell whether this initiative will be successful. I believe that there will be some success stories to come out of the program—participants will receive their associate degrees, hopefully, in concentrations where there is a market for their skills—and find better-paying jobs. What happens, then, when the degree selected becomes obsolete in five years? Will the learner be once again motivated to go back to school to reskill so soon—and this time, without guaranteed assistance from the government? They are back where they started. Yes, a degree is important, but it's also vital that this degree be in a field that will not disappear in less than a decade.

In Iowa, education administrators have recognized for quite some time that learning digital technology skills can lead to a more prosperous future. It was one of the first states in the country to get residents to enroll in programs that will lead to high-demand, tech-based jobs like cybersecurity. Touting over twenty years of experience studying and implementing a fully integrated educational approach, Iowa seems to recognize that teaching data science and cybersecurity cannot simply begin at the university level—there must be a holistic focus on providing the right kinds of opportunities in elementary school. This is great if you live in Iowa, but what about the other forty-nine states? Further, data on how well this program has performed remains elusive, if it ever got off the ground—as of 2017, the program was still in the planning stages, and legislation to compel all Iowa K-12 schools to provide computer science coursework failed in the Iowa Senate. Though it appears that many higher-education institutions in the Hawkeye State have taken the cyber initiative seriously, the early-education component remains shaky.

Meanwhile, the educational system in Texas is working with businesses to create a sustainable digital vocational program, and Divergence is part of it. The Information Technology Registered Apprenticeship program is a state-run career pathway that connects employers and jobseekers through a combination of paid work experience and classroom instruction. These programs range from three to five years and provide a lifeline to individuals looking to train for high-skill, in-demand jobs. Currently, there are 1,300 businesses participating in the program, including Divergence, but the focus until recently has been on traditional jobs like construction and industry and has only recently shifted focus to the technology sector. Still, as of 2018, over 17,500 apprentices are taking advantage of these programs in Texas, with nearly 40 percent training as electricians.

Texas is making these investments in apprenticeships in large part because of the growing recognition that apprenticeships provide a modern model for learning, but the program must grow to include the skills necessary in the twenty-first century. Currently, Divergence is the only school in Texas to both offer courses in cyber and artificial intelligence and facilitate apprenticeships with businesses looking to build up their cyber workforce. That said, Divergence is located at the center of a growing tech hub in the TOLA (Texas, Oklahoma, Louisiana, Arkansas) corridor. Many of the companies in TOLA are recognizable names: Walmart, ExxonMobil, Tyson Foods, Proctor & Gamble, Toyota, Boeing. Though hardly what you think of as tech startups, these companies and many more like them are coming to increasingly rely on cybersecurity tools and artificial intelligence to power their businesses. Companies are moving to Bentonville, Arkansas, just so that they can provide Walmart with supply logistics, much of which requires automation and rapid deployment of digital tools. And Divergence is right in the middle of this expansion, providing talent to help these companies grow their teams.

Up until March 2020, Divergence was able to meet the needs of our learners and our employment partners in-person. That's all been upended by the coronavirus pandemic, but we've been able to continue full steam ahead. Compounding the conundrum currently facing learners of all ages in the post-Covid era has been the blindingly fast shift to online learning. As already discussed, stay-at-home orders extended to school systems, with some districts more prepared than others. Divergence dealt with the shutdown orders with remarkable speed, in large part because my school was built to pivot on a dime, so to speak. Part of what puts Divergence a step ahead of our fellow academic institutions is that I knew before we opened our doors that digital technology would rule our teaching methods. Prior to the pandemic, our class offerings were all conducted in-person on our campus in Addison, Texas, where we had already done away with the "one-size-fits-all" educational approach in favor of a personalized learning experience.

Actively engaging in differentiated learning allows my team to help learners achieve their best outcomes. This may sound intuitive enough, but it's a surprisingly new school of thought.

Personalization as an academic process involves addressing both the strengths and needs of each learner. This is generally achieved by carefully monitoring a learner's progress using clearly identified benchmarks. As such, personalization strives to ensure that the learner's needs are being met. That means meeting emotional and physical needs in tandem with academic ones.

In many traditional schools throughout the United States, individualization often takes a back seat to other priorities, such as ensuring that most learners are meeting grade-level standards. Personalized learning is generally considered the bastion of special education programs in the K-12 system, where Individualized Education Programs (IEP) are created for children eligible for such offerings. Under federal law, an IEP cannot be written until a disability is determined and special education or related services are necessary. Unfortunately, those services disappear at the university level.

A recent RAND Education study sponsored by the Bill and Melinda Gates Foundation found early evidence that personalized learning "can improve achievement for students, regardless of their starting level of achievement." The study also emphasized the importance of technology in achieving better learner outcomes:

> Technology can play a role in supporting the complexity of the personalization process. When properly supported by teachers, it can help students learn independently and work at their own pace. Technology can also enable educators to take a more personalized approach in their teaching efforts and other activities they undertake to support

student learning and development.[2]

Divergence provides learners with the right kinds of opportunities to help them achieve success. To do that, we consider learners' backgrounds and their interests. Further, if we know what interests our learners beyond the classroom, we can find new ways to motivate them when the going gets tough. By taking these factors into consideration, Divergence instructors adapt to the needs of our learners, meeting them in a true personalized engagement. This intensive approach provides the holistic infrastructure needed to succeed. In short, the better we know our students, the better we can adjust to their needs. As I mentioned above, learner outcomes deteriorate when their basic needs are not being met, whether that's being able to afford tuition or transportation to and from campus. And because our school is still on the small side, we are capable of providing housing assistance and other needs. Ensuring our learners are healthy and energized for school will maximize their success.

Who We Serve

Hugh Champs (name changed) knew he needed a change. Facing his fortieth birthday, Hugh felt he hadn't yet lived up to his potential. Until recently, he had bounded around from one low-wage job to another, usually sticking around until boredom set in. One day he was walking by the Divergence campus in Addison and saw that we were enrolling new students. On a whim, he decided to come in and see what we were about.

"I'm looking for a new start—something that will give me the skills I need for a better job," Hugh said to me. "I don't want to be flipping burgers for the rest of my life, but I don't know what my next step should be."

I explained how a job in the technology industry could be just the thing he was looking for. At first, Hugh scoffed.

"Like those guys in Silicon Valley?" he asked. "How am I going to do that? I've never taken any tech classes before, and I'm nearly forty. Aren't I too old?"

"Not at all," I said. "Divergence is a vocational school for the twenty-first century. The skills we teach here are specifically for jobs in the tech field, which now touches nearly every industry on the planet. Think about it: Is there any company that doesn't have some kind of digital component?"

Hugh thought about it for a moment. "That makes sense—if a company hasn't gone digital in some way, it may as well not exist. But where do I fit in?"

"Every one of these companies needs employees who can perform systems checks, data management, and enforce cybersecurity. I can teach you those skills, and I can do it in less than three months. What do you say?"

Hugh was intrigued, but there remained one more issue. "How am I going to pay for this? How am I going to get to school every day? I don't have a car. I don't have a computer. Maybe this isn't the right fit for me. Besides, how will I know that there will even be a job for me at the end of this? What if it's a waste of time?"

"Don't worry. We've got a plan that will work for you, and we will help you find a job."

It turned out that Hugh needed more than a laptop and transportation—he needed a roof over his head and clothes on his back. My team made sure he had all those things so that he could focus on the Divergence bootcamp. Now, clearly, not every student is going to require the same amount of support that Hugh did, but he was driven to complete the program and I wanted to ensure that he could. We could have simply covered Hugh's tuition and said, "Ok, you're on your own from here on out," but that would not have set him up for success.

Housing insecurity can pose enormous obstacles to learners who find themselves having to choose between attending class or completing assignments, and securing a roof over their heads for the night. Studies show that housing insecure students, on average, achieve lower graduation rates in the K-12 system as well as at the two-year and four-year college level. And the problem is more widespread than many of us may realize: research conducted at the University of Massachusetts, Boston found that 45 percent of participants reported housing insecurity.[3] These students are a far cry from the stereotypical "broke college student" subsisting on ramen and Sprite to build up mental fortitude—homelessness and housing insecurity is far more complex and is often hidden due to shame and social stigma. Hugh, and many other learners like him, need the support of student affairs administrators and others in academia to have a chance at success. Knowing that, I decided from the get-go that Divergence would not just pay idle lip service to the problem, but would actually generate change. In fact, one of our students, Patricia Adams, researched the issue of generational poverty and street level homelessness for one of her capstone projects. The challenges facing would-be learners who are homeless are far more nuanced than lack of adequate housing, and her project helped me and my team better understand the situation and tailor our responses as necessary.

We succeed when we empower our learners with the tools needed to land a job. People can move forward if provided opportunity, support, and guidance. And since moving forward requires embracing challenges, we commit to our learners by providing the best industry knowledge, the most up-to-date information, and the most relevant employment resources.

Beyond content and curriculum, my team and I understand the importance of personal wellness and mental health. We do provide a few wrap-around services—protein bars and bananas in common areas, occasional weekly lunches—as well as on-demand access to a local chaplain. When students need more support that we can provide, such as housing and transportation, we reach out to the Dallas Community Council. This is a period of tremendous transition and growth, and we want to make sure our learners are as prepared as possible. The only ingredient we can't bring to the recipe is motivation.

We take on these responsibilities with the expectation that Divergence Academy learners will then be able to meet the demands of our coursework. In practice, that means learners must show up to each class on time and be willing to participate in discussions. They must take agency for their learning because ultimately, no one else can learn the material for them. I can provide all the support in the world, but learners must be ready to put in the time and cultivate the right mindset.

What happened to Hugh? He completed our ten-week bootcamp, earned two certifications in cybersecurity, and is actively on the hunt for a new job. Our talent development officers helped Hugh polish up his resume and create a LinkedIn profile—two steps he never had to take for his old jobs.

When Hugh graduated, he made sure to call his mother and get her to the ceremony. She was so proud. Hugh had an air of accomplishment, of "I've got this." His demeanor was so noticeable that I pulled him aside after graduation to gauge how he was feeling.

"I have never felt like I had control over my future," Hugh said as he beamed a radiant smile. "I always thought I had to take what was offered—and most of those jobs stunk. Now I *know* I have skills that can help me achieve greater possibilities."

Divergence finds itself at the intersection of AI, cloud, and data science, and these domains generate in-demand tech careers that, as I hope I have illustrated, will not become obsolete any time soon. They offer opportunities to repeatedly improve your income and advance your interests.

Most importantly, they require skills that can be learned virtually.

Now that all our classes are remote due to the pandemic,

Divergence learners benefit from dual engagement models known in the education world as remote synchronous learning and asynchronous learning—here's what that means:

In a remote synchronous learning environment, live classes are accessed remotely via Microsoft Teams. Live engagement provides expert instruction with immediate feedback. We are now even exploring implementing hologram technology to replicate the in-person teacher experience. Conversely, when learners are unable to attend virtual or in-person live classes, they can access recordings remotely on their own time. This is asynchronous learning, where flexibility permits more agency in determining the pathway that's best for them.

Though we prefer synchronous learning for many of our courses simply because the live element cannot be easily replicated, asynchronous education offers tremendous benefits. A major concern with this methodology is whether learners are completing their assignments or if they're logging in and zoning out. Someone figured out how to handle that: Carnegie Mellon researcher Ken Koedinger built an intelligent tutoring system that monitors student progress. Further, this intelligent tutoring system is itself an opportunity to learn how to code a computer program that learners might encounter upon graduating from Divergence.

Our goal at Divergence Academy is to improve the overall learning experience, which requires smaller classroom sizes to facilitate individualized attention. Our instructors organize student-to-student engagement through regular virtual small groups using sub-channels on Microsoft Teams. These small groups are entirely led by students and foster the development of technical skills and the often neglected but equally important "soft skills" like decision-making and team collaboration. Personalized learning as a concept is hardly new or innovative. Many academic institutions worldwide have successfully implemented this model—look at the now century-old Montessori method, where self-directed learning is the preferred mode of education, as opposed to forcing students to passively gaze upon the so-called sage on the stage.

Quintan Gee is a recent graduate who started a bootcamp at Divergence in the middle of the pandemic. Prior to Divergence, Quintan had spent four years in the payroll tax department for a Texas-based company, where he quickly rose to a senior position in his department. "I picked it up really quick," he explained. "But there wasn't a lot of room to grow." No raises, for example, and the job quickly turned degrading. "It frustrates me when I tell people that I have an MBA and they say, 'Wow,' like they're surprised a Black man could do that." After fighting for an adjustment in his compensation, "I ended up on medical leave because this incident was so traumatic for me."

At that point, Quintan, at the ripe old age of 34, knew he needed a change. Clearly excelling at taking charge of a situation and learning on the go, he started looking into education programs where he could grow his skills. He looked at a free program in nearby Dallas but it wasn't the right fit. "Once I heard about Divergence, I called for more information. I wanted to do it, but the price was a concern. I was afraid I couldn't do it." Luckily, Beth L. told him about the Texas Workforce Commission and how he could apply for funds to cover the bootcamp. He qualified and started classes. By then, we were six months into the pandemic, and Quintan was about to embark on an intensive bootcamp program.

"It was very intense," he explained. "The program was good. Each week there was literally a new course with new material. I am so glad that everything was recorded so that I could go back after class and review it." A typical day for Quintan started at nine in the morning. "Depending on the instructor, each class would start with a quick review before jumping into new content." There were no surprises about what lay ahead, either. "They had a plan for us. PowerPoint slides, labs, exercises for us to complete." Lunch at noon, then back to class until six.

Quintan's cohort was composed of him and nine other students. And despite being remote, he and his team developed a camaraderie where they leaned on each other in study sessions and turned to one another when they needed to blow off steam. In fact, he said, "I wish we had more group work. But we really bonded with each other." Now, Quintan is building his resume and applying for careers in tech services. He is confident that this program was worthwhile. "I am a little bit nervous because this is a completely new field of expertise, but I am a quick learner, so I know that, once I'm out there, I am going to do it. I am confident I will get a job and will be able to financially take care of myself and my family. I'm a hard worker. I have the skills. I just need the opportunity to prove myself." I know Quintan will do just that, and I cannot wait to see where his career takes him.

As we move forward in a post-Covid landscape, the use of online educational platforms and emerging technologies will permanently support personalized learning in virtual, collaborative classrooms. As many American institutions of higher education were forced to turn to online learning and embrace digital technology, those who failed to pivot quickly revealed deepening cracks in academia.

A study in the June 2020 issue of the Harvard Business Review called for a "New Higher Ed Agenda" wherein academic administrators accept that the trifecta of crushing student debt, skyrocketing tuition, and the rise of digital education platforms is forcing traditional schools to adapt or possibly disappear. "University leaders must use what they are learning in crisis now to position their institutions for greatest impact in the decades to come," Vijay Govindarajan and Anup Srivastava write in their post-mortem analysis of failed education systems post-pandemic. "That means using data now from the current forced online learning experiment and initiating small pilots during the next academic year to test future higher education models." Their suggestions include revisiting the existing residential model, integrate better hybrid options, and build fully online education programs that are as good as what students receive in-person on campus. Time and actual enrollment figures will tell soon enough who heeds these lessons and who doesn't.

As I mentioned previously, I want Divergence to be prepared to teach both humans and robots. I believe that society will be in a position in less than five years where robots will be performing asynchronous work and capable of independent thought beyond simple decision-making. In fact, I think we're already there. Boston Dynamics is a Massachusetts-based technology company that manufactures mobile robots. One of its earliest mobile robots was Spot, a yellow, four-legged canine-inspired robot that climbs stairs and covers rugged terrain at a top speed of three miles per hour. According to the company, Spot was designed to go "where wheeled robots cannot, while carrying payloads with endurance far beyond aerial drones. With 360-degree vision and obstacle avoidance, the robot can be driven remotely or taught routes and actions to perform autonomous missions."[4] Boston Dynamics envisions Spot working at heavy construction sites, inspecting operations at oil and gas facilities and delivering food and medicine.

Boston's Brigham and Women's Hospital began employing Spot in March 2020 to help reduce frontline healthcare workers' exposure to Covid-19. Boston Dynamics foresees further implementation of Spot in the healthcare sector and envisions the robot triaging sick patients, which requires outfitting Spot with the capability to take body temperature, respiratory rate, pulse rate, and oxygen saturation—in other words, to equip Spot with the skills and tools commonly employed by frontline healthcare nurses. Soon, scientists expect they will be able to train Spot to disinfect spaces needing decontamination, such as hospital tents or subway stations. "We hope our fellow mobile robot providers, existing customers, and medical professionals will be able to use this information to leverage mobile robots to take people out of harm's way during this critical time. Together, we can improve conditions for healthcare workers and essential personnel around the world, save lives, and fight COVID-19," concludes a Boston Dynamic press release. These last two sentences support my belief that humans will remain essential in this relationship.

Robots are nothing without their creators—even the mighty humanoid robot Atlas, also created by Boston Dynamics and capable of leaping and jogging without following a preprogrammed route, needed computer data specialists and robotics experts to get it off the drawing board. In fact, one of the most critical jobs now involves training those robots to work alongside their human counterparts. Consider the massive multinational aerospace and defense manufacturer Raytheon Technologies, whose 47,000-square-foot factory in Tucson, Arizona is a textbook example of humans and robots working together, side by side. Yes, Raytheon is most definitely building robots for going into battlefields and making on-the-ground decisions that evolve with field conditions, but in Tucson, the company wanted more commonplace robots to perform mundane, repetitive tasks safely alongside people. No, Raytheon did not build these robots, but after the run-of-the-mill robots arrived, Raytheon scientists swapped out the manufacturer's software for a simpler after-market program that makes training and retraining the robots easier for their human handlers. These robots are ideal for completing repetitive tasks such as assembly line work and are unlikely to succumb to human error. And that's particularly important for a company that makes high-precision items like rockets and missiles.

Low-level robots are ideal for mundane tasks that require a high degree of precision, saving the more complex, higher-level thinking jobs for humans. Further, those robots do need maintenance and regular updates to their software. *Those* are the jobs for which we need to prepare the next generation of workers. Assembly line drudgery is being taken over by machines, but that frees up living, breathing workers to tackle more challenging work, much of which will include maintaining robots, keeping them clean of malware and cybersecurity attacks, and performing other technical critical thinking jobs requiring the human touch.

The robot-work equation continues to be examined by companies like Rethink Robotics, a startup that created robots to work collaboratively with humans. Though now-defunct, the Boston-based firm founded by iRobot creator and MIT robotics professor Rodney Brooks focused on developing "cobots"— small, easily-programmable robots designed to work alongside people on factory floors—and for about a decade it was one of the pioneering startups in next-generation robotics engineering. Unlike other, more industrial robots deemed too dangerous to work side-by-side with humans, Rethink Robotics focused on creating safe and reliable robots. Ultimately, Rethink was unable to stay afloat because it failed to accurately predict what the market wanted and closed its doors in 2018—such is the cutthroat life cycle of startups in the digital age.

Though the era of collaborative robots may be off to a bumpy start, other companies, like Denmark-based startup Universal Robots, have learned from Rethink's mistakes and are making huge gains in the market. The business of building collaborative robots is only in its infancy, and these companies are creating machines intended to work alongside people rather than displace their human counterparts completely. As MIT professor Rodney Brooks said, improving robotic technology is not meant to eradicate people; rather, employed intelligently, robots may free us up to achieve greater things: "I see robotic technology getting rid of the dangerous, the dirty, and the just plain boring jobs," Brooks said. "Some people say, 'You can't. People won't have anything to do.' But we [humanity] found things that were a lot easier than backbreaking labor in the sun and fields. Let people rise to do better things."[5]

With this in mind, we must be aware that one major fallout from the Covid crisis will be that many jobs lost during the pandemic will come back, but not for humans; robotic butlers and assembly-line robots are on the job. Again, the rise of the robots is nothing new—scientists and researchers have been predicting this for decades—but now we are seeing in real time how vital it is for people to get retrained and reskilled in new jobs.

And yes, states like Michigan and Iowa are offering free tuition to workers who want to get retrained, but state budgets are always in flux, and post-pandemic, you can be sure that education funding will be cut in an effort to save money. Federal funds and grants do exist to help learners achieve further education but some of these funds are ineligible for programs like bootcamps. Gabe Dalporto, CEO of online data science program Udacity, painted a far more dire picture than even what most scientists have: "A billion people will lose their jobs over the next ten years due to AI, and if anything, COVID has accelerated that by about nine years. If you tried to reskill a billion people in the university system, you would break the university system."

Where do we go from here? In the future, AI and robotics will be seamless elements of society, and we will be expected to play an active role in making sure our technology does not fail us. As Norbert Wiener wrote in Cybernetics in 1948, "The world of the future will be an even more demanding struggle against the limitations of our intelligence, not a comfortable hammock in which we can lie down to be waited upon by our robot slaves."

CHAPTER SIX

Speak Softly and Carry a Big Stick

The looming threat of mass Structural Unemployment is everyone's problem. Nearly half of the country could be affected directly and the rest could suffer from the consequences of a devastated U.S. economy. Many people fail to realize that it won't just be factory workers and unskilled laborers who lose their jobs. Technology is eliminating highly skilled positions in white-collar industries as well.

Art Bilger, Founder & CEO, WorkingNation

Structural unemployment has been looming on the horizon for years, but the focus has largely been on those blue-collar and unskilled workers whose jobs are being taken over by digital technologies—and as venture capitalist Art Bilger points out above, that's hardly the case. AI and other digital technologies are coming for a lot of middle class and white-collar jobs, too. As someone who focuses on the future of work and the skills gap, Bilger has been outspoken for years about the importance of integrating digital technologies with work, digital media, and online education.

The employment crisis Bilger began exploring back in 2016 is happening now, not ten years from now. "There's a gap between the skills employers need from their workers, both now and in the future, and the skills Americans actually have. The equation is not pretty," Bilger writes. "Our education system hasn't kept up with the rapidly changing skills needed as technology plays a larger role in jobs of all kinds." As I hope I have demonstrated throughout, Bilger's prognostications are bearing fruit—our traditional education system is failing to keep up with the pace of change, and the American worker will bear the brunt of the pain—that is, if that worker remains unskilled and unequipped to meet the challenges ahead. It is my goal to provide the right skills to create productive members of the new work force.

But systemic change is slow—what an institution does in one state may vary widely from its counterparts elsewhere. Public education systems are influenced by ever-fluctuating budgets while politicians find themselves at the mercy of public sentiment and the next voting cycle, rather than sound judgment. Though large-scale change is necessary, public institutions and massive private corporations are bogged down and inert by design. Innovative solutions are more likely to come from smaller, more agile corners of our economy, such as startups and next-gen companies like my own.

The tech revolution is here, and for all of us to succeed within it, we must understand what that change means, as well as the roles we must assume to be successful. Look, the one percent will be fine—they have enough money and resources to survive the various economic and environmental changes underway, but the rest of us need to accept the cold truth that this change is happening blazing fast, and if we don't keep up, we will be left behind, unemployed, unskilled, and at the mercy of the new order. We must be willing to retool and develop a sense of self-reliance to remain balanced in a world where progress will happen seemingly overnight. And we cannot do it alone—we've got to help each other out.

Certain types of jobs are now being completed by AI and robots. The jobs that humans will perform, now and in the future, will focus on problem-solving and require high-cognitive abilities. Jobs offering better pay and some semblance of stability will require workers to think and persuade. That means lawyers dealing in complex litigation are going to be secure, while attorneys who only do document review are probably going to want to look for another skill. To avoid being disenfranchised by the new tech world order, workers must be willing to rethink their roles and accept that the job market of yore no longer exists.

Manual labor will be delegated to robots and low-wage earners without skills. The great divide will be found in the middle class, where traditional jobs like bank tellers, legal secretaries, parking enforcers, and data entry technicians are being lost to efficiencies gained by technology. "Job polarization," as it's called, has been discussed by scientists since the 1950s and is inextricably linked to the shift from manufacturing to services and automation. Americans didn't begin to truly feel the pinch, however, until the 1980s, and even then, the scope was limited to blue-collar jobs.

As a country founded on the principles of a middle-class nation, where people work and contribute to a society that will support them when the going gets tough, this shift I'm talking about will require change and adaptation at every level, a system-wide reassessment of public policies while finally addressing the fact that middle-class workers have been falling behind in wage growth for over forty years. If left unresolved, the future looks even dimmer for working class Americans, those whom Brookings Institution researcher Isabel Sawhill calls the "forgotten Americans" and who make up 38 percent of the working age population. These are the people most in need of retooling to face the future of work.[1]

Don't be fooled: your job as you know it is not immune. A study conducted at Oxford University examined 702 specific occupations and how susceptible they are to computerization and automation. After approximately fifty pages of mathematical calculations, the findings are sobering:

> While computerisation has been historically confined to routine tasks involving explicit rule-based activities, algorithms for big data are now rapidly entering domains reliant upon pattern recognition and can readily substitute for labour in a wide range of non-routine cognitive tasks. In addition, advanced robots are gaining enhanced senses and dexterity, allowing them to perform a broader scope of manual tasks.
>
> According to our estimates around 47 percent of total US employment is in the high risk category. We refer to these

> as jobs at risk – i.e., jobs we expect could be automated relatively soon, perhaps over the next decade or two .... More surprisingly, we find that a substantial share of employment in service occupations, where most US job growth has occurred over the past decades, are highly susceptible to computerisation. Additional support for this finding is provided by the recent growth in the market for service robots and the gradually diminishment of the comparative advantage of human labour in tasks involving mobility and dexterity.... Our findings thus imply that as technology races ahead, low-skill workers will reallocate to tasks that are non-susceptible to computerisation – i.e., tasks requiring creative and social intelligence. For workers to win the race, however, they will have to acquire creative and social skills.[2]

This study concludes with an appendix rating those 702 occupations from least likely to most likely to becoming automated. Physical therapists, dieticians, dentists, and teachers were among those least likely to see their jobs replaced by automation; but telemarketers, tax preparers, clerks of various kinds, sports officials, cashiers, real estate agents, pharmacy technicians, refuse collectors, and insurance sales agents will see their jobs relegated to machines much sooner than they may realize.

Ok, so I've convinced you, I hope, that change is afoot and that the workforce must retool via appropriate education programs. Some schools market their offerings as a way to get ahead in the job market, but at steep costs and without any actual assurances of finding a job at the end of it. If you're reasonably well-heeled, maybe taking that kind of risk is OK, but how many times will you want to go back for another degree? After a while, the costs will add up. My school, by contrast, focuses on those most likely to get left behind in the groundswell—notably, veterans and those from underserved communities—by offering transferable skill sets even as the work itself will change.

As I discussed earlier, retrained and reskilled veterans offer tremendous benefits to society, and some even go back to the military as reservists to work on cybersecurity and artificial intelligence. I'm helping them achieve job security through Divergence, which I want to become the best vocational trade school dedicated to technology. Focusing on emerging technologies—which currently include cyber, edge computing, the internet of things, and AI—puts my students at the vanguard of the employment sphere. Remember, conceptually, emerging technologies will always include the latest digital wizardry, and so by default that means that an emerging technology will change. Once upon a time, electricity was an emerging technology—you get my point. What won't change is the need for employers to find skilled workers capable of negotiating the new world. Divergence is that bridge between the two.

The Divergence curriculum is agile and made to adapt as technology evolves. Though we launched as a bootcamp-style intensive, Divergence has evolved to include new kinds of programs to complement our bootcamp models, specifically towards providing end-to-end, turnkey solutions to employers in the form of a skilled workforce. We are also actively generating awareness of the federal government's research and development tax credit, a solution that can encourage small businesses to innovate and train their workers with new skills. Many companies are eligible to take advantage of this credit but don't realize it. The benefits of doing so are remarkable, especially for those looking to expand their tech and research capabilities. According to section 41 of the Internal Revenue Code, the following four-part test must be met in full to qualify:

1. Be intended to "discover information that would eliminate uncertainty concerning the development or improvement of a project;"

2. Rely on "principles of the physical or biological sciences, engineering, or computer science;"

3. Relate to the development of "a new or improved business component of the taxpayer;"

4. Include a "'process of experimentation test,' which requires that qualified research be research 'substantially all of the activities of which constitute elements of a process of experimentation.'"

In plain English, companies looking to innovate and employ cutting-edge technologies are eligible for research and development tax credits from the government. That could apply to wages paid to employees engaged in research, supplies, contractor expenses, and—most importantly for our purposes—education providers. In fact, any expenditures made for education purposes can be covered at 75 percent of the actual cost.

At Divergence, I can use those credits to innovate and grow my business. For example, I've created Divergence Labs, where my team and I are innovating how we deliver, create, and distribute content through augmented reality, virtual reality, mixed reality, and other distribution mechanisms. The tax credit gives us the latitude to improve our offerings and then actually teach what goes on in those labs as standalone courses. It is a self-perpetuating cycle of learning through making, and this tax credit helps us achieve that.

Time spent in the lab is hands-on work, all in the service of our primary goal of getting our learners employed once they finish our program. I believe the best way to create talent that employers want is to demonstrate that we are also consuming that talent. To that end, Divergence employs its own graduates. So, learners complete the program and then some of them come to work for Divergence in security operations, analytics, at the help desk, or in tech support. Now, at first blush, you might argue that these are entry-level type positions, and you would be correct. But every graduate, no matter what institution they hail from, needs to start somewhere.

Everyone needs to get their feet wet in an entry-level position, as well as the confidence necessary to stick with this new job field. Divergence provides the platform for these graduates to test their skills by working with the latest and greatest tech gadgets, then apply for sought-after positions with their newfound and highly marketable skills. We are working on a new model that merges apprenticeships with managed services so that we can bring newer models of generating student experiences.

The Apprentice

Mention apprenticeships to most learners and employers, and you may get more than one quizzical response. *Didn't apprenticeships disappear in the nineteenth century? I thought that was a reality tv show. But in real life? No way. Shouldn't we be focusing on internships instead?* Though it may sound old-fashioned, an apprenticeship-based learn and earn model is at the vanguard of fusing work and education in the twenty-first century. And since postsecondary education is, on the whole, disengaged with the contemporary workforce, potential employees need to find a better way to upskill and get hired. The digital age requires a new way for American workers to find quality jobs without running up thousands of dollars in student loan debt. Apprenticeships, also commonly referred to as "active learning," are probably as disruptive to the traditional internship or entry-level working program as massive open online courses (MOOCs) were to academia. Apprentice-based programs are the successful modern method of incubating workforce training, and yet, the concept is downright medieval in origin.

You don't have to take my word for it: Look at the apprenticeship models currently in place in Finland, Germany, and France. Vocational education and training (VET) in these countries grew out of the medieval craft guilds, in which training and education were passed from master to apprentice. Some positions were more coveted than others, and placement in particularly well-connected apprenticeships could secure higher social status and better economic footing. After completing what was often a years-long program, recruits would be welcomed into the craft or trade guild as a lifetime member. Such programs were exclusionary by design, and powerful guilds flexed their muscle by preventing outsiders from entering a trade. Wealthy families could buy apprenticeships for their children, thereby excluding those who might also have the talent and acumen to participate, but not necessarily the funds to compete. (Sounds a lot like how some kids get into colleges these days, doesn't it? Some things never change.)

By the 1800s, the Industrial Revolution disrupted the traditional guild model throughout Europe, and modern assembly-line jobs greatly reduced the need for skilled labor. Some countries didn't let the concept totally die, however, and some foreword-thinking organizers and politicians had the wherewithal and support to see that apprenticeships held the keys to sustainable growth.

If we learn anything from history, it would be that over one hundred years ago, Finnish leaders recognized the divide between the wealthy and the vast underclass of unskilled and underskilled laborers. The existing system was not sufficiently training the Finnish workforce to compete in the modern economy, and the root cause lay squarely in the education model.

Rather than throw money at the problem, ignore it, or apply a salve, Finnish leaders took up the charge of fundamentally changing the existing model. Vocational education was nationalized and institutionalized in the nineteenth century, and schools were established throughout the country and exhaustive in scope:

> Vocational education was needed to provide students with good vocational skills because the existing formal educational system concentrated only on the education of civil servants and civilized people. The need to change and reorganize vocational education became recognized as essential....Schooling for seafaring started in 1813, and schooling for health care and midwifery in 1816. The first business college was established in 1839, the first agricultural college in 1839, the first technical real colleges in 1847 and the first forestry college in 1861.

Built using models already established in Germany and the Netherlands, the Finnish national undertaking was a pioneer in vocational education and training. Further, the Finnish education did not require four years of basic education to participate in these apprenticeships (though that requirement would change in the 1930s). Then, as now, vocational education proved essential to meet the needs of working with new technologies. Remember, emerging technologies were once electricity and automated machinery. Today, it's fiberoptics and AI.

The Finnish apprenticeship model did not disappear with the twentieth century; rather, it has once again been remodeled and retrofitted to meet contemporary needs. A reform undertaken in the 1960s and 70s revised and improved the VET program by creating new specializations. After some ups and downs in the intervening years, vocational education in Finland has been almost uniformly incorporated into society. As professors Stenstrom and Virolainen point out in their history of Finnish vocational training, the results are overwhelmingly positive:

> On-the-job learning is guided and goal-oriented study at the workplace. Since the system has been introduced, there has been a persistent declining trend in the number of dropouts from initial VET....Studies have shown that vocational students have been motivated to learn 'real work' during their workplace learning periods. In particular, students have felt that they have learnt independency and initiative taking and have become more self-confident. With respect to adopting professional, learning, collaboration, and self-assessment skills, they consider themselves as having developed as professional agents more generally.[3]

The Finnish model is hardly ad hoc, but the product of a nationally regulated program. Students apply through a national application, and qualifications are judged on competence-based exams and other requirements. In other words, there's no one-size-fits-all SAT-type test to gain admission—something else American schools are only just now beginning to recognize.

The vocational model has overtaken traditional apprenticeships in popularity, but the Finnish Ministry of Education has focused on regulating and streamlining the more artisanal version as well by introducing various initiatives through the twentieth century to encourage the adoption of general principles across employers. As of 2012, the apprenticeship model has grown, but on its own has not seen the same kind of robust interest as the larger VET program and has become more of a bespoke initiative rather than the robust skills-training force that the VET provides.

While the Finnish model boasts a robust history, the German Vocational Training System is considered the international standard for how a systematic and fully integrated training system can function. Also known as the dual system, this vocational program is fully embedded within the existing German educational system and has been regulated by the Federal Government since 1969.[4] And the "dual-system" is precisely that: programs range from two to four years, during which participants split their time between classroom instruction and the company sponsoring their apprenticeship. These programs don't provide free labor either—apprentices are paid for their work in and out of the classroom—and jockeying for spots is fierce; the ratio of available positions to worthy applicants can be as competitive as getting into an Ivy League college.

By mandating cooperation between companies and vocational schools, student learners acquire relevant education and training for jobs in every industry in Germany. In fact, over 330 occupations, from sales assistants and electricians, to aviation services specialists and shoe manufacturers, require the completion of a vocational training program. All the major internationally-known German companies like Daimler and Bosch participate in apprenticeship programs, too. Fully 60 percent of young people in Germany train as apprentices—compared with a paltry five percent here in the United States.

Part of what allows the German model to succeed is that the training and certification programs are standardized throughout the country—so, the training a computer technician apprentice receives in Hamburg will be identical to a program offered in Munich. The certifications resulting from these programs provide reliable proof to would-be employers that the apprentice participated in a recognized and federally regulated program. Further, the requirements for these apprenticeship programs are regularly updated to address technological advances and innovation within each industry. The German model is so solid that, since 2013, the country has led the development of similar programs in Greece, Portugal, Italy, Slovakia, and Latvia.[5]

An article appearing in *The Atlantic* in 2014 explored, among other things, why the apprenticeship model remains so successful in Germany. Part of the reason is that employers don't look down their noses at apprentices as practitioners of menial labor. "Building world-class diesel parts is hard. We're very careful about who we hire. We're looking for quality," said a hiring manager at Bosch.[6] That perception simply doesn't exist in as many industries in the United States—at least, not yet.

France, like many other European countries, also claims a long history with apprentices, which are defined by the government as "a 'young professional' who follows a training that draws on an alternation of work-based (in-company) training and school-based training." Currently, there are two officially sanctioned apprenticeship models in France: the "apprenticeship contract" and the "professionalization contract." The former has existed since 1919, while the professionalization contract was created in 2004. Both were established to address chronic youth unemployment and focus heavily on vocational training. Officially sanctioned apprenticeships include a mix of hands-on work and education, with a minimum of 400 hours spent at a licensed apprenticeship center.

As in Germany and Finland, all the major companies with some connection to France engage in the VET model, from Airbus to Hermès, as well as thousands of small businesses across the country like bakeries and hair salons. France's model is widely regarded as one of the best anywhere on the planet and one of the Macron administration's quiet victories. During the depths of the coronavirus pandemic, the French government pledged to spend an additional one billion euros to increase apprentice partnerships. As part of that spending program, the French government increased its stipend to each apprentice as a way to encourage companies to keep these workers employed.

And still, the French government feels there's room for improvement, especially among young people who see apprenticeships as a waste of time. Policy changes are important but getting engagement and buy-in from the community is what matters most. You can run an outstanding program, but you're toast if no one believes in it. The French model is good, but it could be better—and the government is pouring substantial resources into it to ensure that it meets their goals of building a dexterous and educated workforce.

Though there is a history of apprenticeship in the United States—Benjamin Franklin was an apprentice in his brother's printshop—there is currently no nationally orchestrated vocational education program or apprenticeship program. Nonetheless, the Department of Labor provides some guidance to those interested in pursuing such an endeavor, defining it as when a worker receives a minimum of 2,000 hours of on-the-job training, a minimum of 144 classroom hours, and the worker is provided a wage for the duration of the program. And yet, apprenticeships in America remain underutilized; according to think tank Third Way, only 5,000 Americans complete apprenticeships annually.[7] Part of the lack of enthusiasm stems from the fact that the current apprentice model as practiced in the United States is outdated and pegged to blue-collar jobs in manufacturing and transportation. A study conducted by the Harvard Business School found that "of the 810 occupations identified by the U.S. Department of Labor, 27 make up the core of apprenticeships in the United States."[8] Clearly, American enterprises would benefit from apprenticeship programs because, though technology has displaced workers, the digital economy also fosters "a highly dynamic technology environment…[and] whole new categories of jobs in the U.S. economy." In other words, there is tremendous potential for the apprenticeship model to work in dozens of industries that pay living wages and offer the opportunity for upward mobility. The missing link in the modern education and workforce gap is for firms to double down on apprenticeships.

Apprentices provide one avenue for business leaders to hire talent—internships, contract-to-hire, and full-time employees are other conduits—but our goal at Divergence is to encourage those companies to look to us as providers of managed employee services via apprenticeships. For example, let's say Microsoft needs help desk support. They can come to us to fill that need. And every company needs back-office tech support. Not only do I find talent, I train them, and in turn, I provide that talent to a company. Since Divergence is a young company, I have to convince these potential hiring partners that an apprenticeship using our graduates is worthwhile, so I put my money where my mouth is and hire my own talent, when appropriate. Divergence becomes a mini-ecosystem where I am both the consumer (hiring apprentices) and producer (teaching students the skills necessary to take on external apprenticeships).

All of this requires innovation, which is helped along by those research and development tax credits and the benefits of being a fleet-footed small business. As a strategy and innovation guy from Microsoft, this is the first time I've been able to apply the techniques I learned there to my own business. The apprentices working in my lab are earning and learning in an outcomes-based program, and upon completion, participants walk away with a certain number of high-value skills that they can transfer to another job.

We incubated our own apprenticeship model and it's begun to bear fruit, especially for our veterans. They are wonderful talent, with focus, energy, perseverance, teamwork, problem-solving skills, and critical thinking. If you teach them IT, they can perform the job. Providing veterans a year or two in an apprenticeship molds them into excellent IT professionals.

Outreach and Enrollment

We have five mechanisms to help us broaden our apprenticeship reach. One is talent placement. Another is talent development, where we upskill and reskill existing employees for corporations. Thirdly, we focus on the future of work and how we need to adapt for it. This dovetails with the future of the classroom—how it will look and how students will learn, both at Divergence and at other institutions—and finally, we advocate for initiatives that include veterans in their hiring plans. I think these areas of focus will be sustainable even as the actual work product or deliverable evolves with each iteration of new technology.

Work is constantly going to change, thanks to the advent of technologies and the future of technology. Every generation brings its own set of opportunities and challenges that we've got to tackle if we're going to succeed.

Innovate or disappear. It's such a simple concept, but it requires a dedication and an understanding that many American companies and schools don't possess. It's easier for a new company like my own to evolve to meet new demand, and I suspect that those institutions who do not evolve will be facing a reckoning in the form of decreased enrollment (and tuition payments) sooner rather than later.

CHAPTER SEVEN
Intelligence Amplification

Man's population and gross product are increasing at a considerable rate, but the complexity of his problems grows still faster, and the urgency with which solutions must be found becomes steadily greater in response to the increased rate of activity and the increasingly global nature of that activity. Augmenting man's intellect... would warrant full pursuit by an enlightened society if there could be shown a reasonable approach and some plausible benefits.

Douglas Engelbart, "Augmenting Human Intellect: A Conceptual Framework" [1962]

The name of the inventor of the word processor, email, and the mouse may not be on the tip of the tongue of the average American, but everyone who has ever used a personal computer in the past thirty years has Douglas Engelbart (1925-2013) to thank for those innovations.

The most significant, perhaps, of Engelbart's advances is the work he completed for the military-focused research and development organization known as Advanced Research Projects Agency (ARPA)—the Eisenhower-era predecessor of today's Defense Advanced Research Projects Agency, or DARPA—where he led the creation of networked digital environments meant to support human-to-human interaction via computers. Among the innovations Engelbart pioneered were concepts that paved the way for the creation of the internet we all know and employ daily. Championing this technology was borne in part by Engelbart's belief that interactive computers would spur humans to scale greater intellectual heights while also serving as a conduit for sharing knowledge at lightning speed. In his 1962 paper, "Augmenting Human Intellect: A Conceptual Framework," Engelbart offers the following hypothetical in which man is aided by computer:

> Let us consider an "augmented" architect at work. He sits at a working station that has a visual display screen some three feet on a side: this is his working surface, and is controlled by a computer (his "clerk") with which he can communicate by means of a small keyboard and other devices.
>
> He is designing a building. He has already dreamed up several basic layouts and structural forms, and is trying them out on the screen. The surveying data for the layout he is working on now have already been entered, and he has just asked his "clerk" to show him a perspective view of the steep hillside building site with the roadway above....A structure is taking shape. He examines it, adjusts it, pauses long enough to ask for a handbook or catalog information from the "clerk" at various points, and readjusts accordingly. He often recalls from the "clerk" his working lists of

> specifications and considerations to refer to them, modify them, or add to them.[1]

The description continues in detail, and to contemporary readers, the exercise sounds downright banal, but in 1962, Engelbart was describing a relationship that could have been pulled from science fiction. Here an architect was not only relying on the assistance of a computer, he was communicating with it. The goal of such interactions, as Engelbart concludes, is not for the computer to supplant the architect, as no doubt many reading this account might think, but so that "the capability of the computer for executing mathematical processes would be used whenever it was needed."

This rapidly approaching future was nothing to fear, Engelbart argued, because humans were already heading in the direction of engaging in more complex cognitive skills, so why not delegate the prosaic and time-consuming tasks to computers? "Every person who does his thinking with symbolized concepts (whether in the form of the English language, formal logic, or mathematics) should be able to benefit significantly." Engelbart's optimistic assertion—that computers will assist rather than replace humans—requires some added context, as the world has evolved greatly since this paper was written, in the middle of the twentieth century. As pointed out in the previous chapter, computers and AI are indeed supplanting people in certain professional domains—even Engelbart's example refers to the architect's computer as "the clerk," ignorant of the reality that though the architect's job is secure, the data entry technician is out of luck—an undeniable oversight.

Engelbart either ignores or disregards the obvious follow-up question that asks, what about all those displaced human clerks? What happens to them?

But policymakers and the average worker should not see this displacement as permanent. It is an opportunity for growth—to achieve Engelbart's belief that humanity is clearly capable of greatness. And yet, it is not a free gift: to take advantage of our innate inner greatness will require us all—corporations, governments, educators, and private citizens—to actively engage with the circumstances surrounding us, rather than waiting on the sidelines, hoping someone will notice and throw us a lifeline.

The Future is Under Construction

The coronavirus pandemic pushed many businesses to make the painful decision to furlough or fire employees. Even the tech sector hemorrhaged tens of thousands of jobs. That in itself will result in less innovation, as startups focusing on AI and other emerging digital tools tighten their belts in a bid to survive until the next round of funding. There's a trickle-down effect going on here as well: larger, more established firms often hire from startups and small tech firms, or even acquire startups outright. Certainly, unemployed tech workers could just as easily take the initiative and apply to jobs at the larger firms, but will they be as likely to be hired if they've been out of work for six months? That's nearly a lifetime in the tech world, and anyone out of the game for that long will have to be incredibly motivated to stay abreast of trends and innovations on their own.

Some of those jobs may return. Others just won't. Plenty of jobs are—or already have—been allocated to robots or AI. The jobs that remain—and those to be created by new advances in technology—will require new skills and an ability to pivot quickly from one task to another. For those employees, reskilling will be the difference between finding gainful employment and waiting on the unemployment line. It's what my team of educators at Divergence focuses on during our all-hands planning meetings and when we're plotting out curricula. But we're a small concern; to truly create large-scale change will require more than one Divergence Academy, and it will require employers to shift their perspectives on how they both hire and train their workers. Unless you run a fast-food shack, the days of hiring and firing entry-level "clerks" is probably over.

The shift is underway as employers are already sensitive to the new technological demands on employees. A survey published by McKinsey and Company in 2018 found that 66 percent of respondents representing a cross-section of employers from the business and public sectors said they believed "addressing potential skills gaps related to automation/digitization was an urgent priority."[2] Add that to an estimated 14 percent of the global workforce—approximately 375 million workers—facing the reality that by 2030 they may have to switch careers because theirs will be taken over by digital technologies, and you've got a pot boiling with no one tending it. Awareness is the first step, but action is critical.

Further, 62 percent of respondents to the McKinsey survey also believed they will need to retrain or replace more than a quarter of their workforce between now and 2023. Comparisons to the shift from agricultural to industrial work are fair, except that this is happening far quicker and may have devastating consequences if not addressed thoughtfully and appropriately. Unfortunately, most corporations and governments are paying little more than lip-service to the scope of what lays ahead.

Ok, retooling and reskilling is important, I hope you are thinking. *How much is it going to cost?* Fair and critical question. The cost to retrain humans to work in the new economy with new technology and alongside robots is considerable, but saves money overall. Harvard Business School professor Joseph Fuller says that companies are "better off growing [their] own [workforce]" rather than engaging in the never-ending cycle of hiring and firing.[3] Research conducted by Professor Matthew Bidwell at the Wharton School of Business likewise revealed that looking outward for new recruits comes at substantial costs. Employees hired from outside a company generally earn "significantly lower performance evaluations for their first two years on the job than do internal workers who are promoted into similar jobs. They also have higher exit rates, and they are paid 'substantially more.' About 18% to 20% more."[4] But those higher paychecks don't result in better workers:

> I found that hires have a significantly lower average performance than workers promoted into the job....External

> hires' higher turnover and termination rates also provide strong evidence of their poorer fit with their jobs....[5]

Another study funded by the Center for American Progress corroborated Bidwell's hypothesis, finding that high business turnover also incurs high retraining costs. In some cases the turnover costs can exceed 213 percent, though the average hovered around 30 percent, still a substantial number for any business to absorb.

In a finding published by the World Economic Forum in 2019, the total cost to the U.S. labor market to reskill workers is $34 billion, but 86 percent of that cost would be likely shouldered by the government.[6] And yet, a study published by the Organization for Economic Co-operation and Development found that the United States spends $50 billion annually on labor market programs, which sounds impressive until you look at that as a percentage of gross domestic product, or GDP, which equals less than half a percent overall.[7] The World Economic Forum further stressed the need for the U.S. government to take this initiative seriously:

> The [U.S.] government could reskill as many as 77% of all at-risk workers, with a clear return on investment coming from increased tax returns and lower social costs such as unemployment compensation. For the remaining 18%, the costs outweigh the economic returns to government, while for 5% a similar-skills and higher-wage pathway is not available.

That 18 percent may not seem like a lot, but in real numbers, that's 252,000 people being relegated to the "untrainable" category.

Since 2017, the World Economic Forum has been advancing a program called "Closing the Skills Gap 2020" which has already secured retraining for 6.4 million people worldwide, and the best results so far have come from public-private partnerships.

Still, in the United States, nearly a quarter of reskilling will be expected to be done by the private sector, equaling approximately 350,000 workers overall. "The ability of the private sector to profitably absorb the reskilling burden could rise to 45% of at-risk workers if businesses collaborate to create economies of scale," the World Economic Forum study finds. Larger, forward-thinking companies have already begun to fund reskilling efforts. Amazon recently announced a $700 million commitment to reskill 100,000 of its workers to help them "gain critical skills to move into higher skill, better paying, technical or non-technical roles" and will focus heavily on cloud computing and machine learning. It even launched its own six-week initiative for Amazon workers to gain coding skills. Microsoft created its own program in June 2020 to help 25 million global citizens acquire new digital skills. In these and other programs, the emphasis is on vocational training as a key factor in skill development.

Now, as for how much this is likely to cost the average corporation, it won't be cheap: the cost of reskilling each American in need is approximately $24,800. Multiply that by the roughly 1.37 million American workers who will be out of work, and you're looking at a hefty sum, but knowing that hiring an external worker can cost six times more than spending a set amount on reskilling, and you're looking at a compelling business case for reskilling. AT&T provides an example of a major firm that looked inward and realized it needed help. An internal investigation launched in 2008 found that half its workforce lacked the necessary skills to navigate digital work requirements. As a result, AT&T concluded that it did not have the talent needed. Further, the Dallas-based telecommunications company found that 100,000 workers were likely to be replaced by automation in the next decade. Senior executive vice president of human resources Bill Blase explained the situation to CNBC:

> We could go out and try to hire all these software and engineering people and probably pay through the nose to get them, but even that wouldn't have been adequate. Or we could try to reskill our existing workforce so they could be competent in the technology and the skills required to run the business going forward.

Unlike the roughly 60 percent of maturing companies in the United States that aren't adequately preparing for the coming digital tsunami, AT&T took action, to the tune of $1 billion. And the company didn't merely throw money at the situation, but structured its efforts across multiple platforms, offering online courses via Coursera and other institutions and creating an internal career center dedicated to helping employees retrain for jobs they want elsewhere in the company.

Ten years after AT&T launched this effort, results are beginning to come in, and they offer reassurance to other companies that haven't yet taken that first step. Half of the firm's employees have enrolled and completed 2.7 million online courses on cybersecurity and data science, and nearly 500 employees have enrolled in a virtual computer science master's degree program through the Georgia Institute of Technology. Retraining and reskilling has helped employees move within the company to better-paying roles and to positions where more in-depth technical knowledge is necessary. Now, rather than hiring expensive contractors, AT&T is looking internally.

Of course, it helps that the C-suite brass were convinced from the outset that investing in reskilling was a strategic move with positive benefits. Also, unlike smaller institutions, AT&T has the massive bandwidth to conduct employee development at scale. Other firms may also have the size but lack the direction or desire to move the needle.

How, then, can other companies make the investment when they don't have the internal structure to do so? As a telecommunications company, AT&T was positioned a few steps ahead, so investing in technology seemed second-nature. But what about Walmart, Home Depot, and other large concerns that aren't necessarily high-tech by design but are relying on digital advancements to run their businesses? For starters, they come to us for help. At Divergence, that means filling knowledge gaps with tailored technology programs that are evolving at the pace of innovation—a nearly impossible task, especially since today's skills will not match tomorrow's jobs. To succeed, companies and governments need to accept that earning a degree or certificate isn't the issue, but that learning in this case is directly in the service of hiring or retraining workers. Also, it shouldn't matter whether a learner earns a degree or a certificate, what matters are the skills they acquire.

Remember our discussion on the soaring costs of four-year college degrees? That's going to be a major deterrent to would-be learners from completing a program unless that degree is both funded by their employer and results in a job. Most of the in-demand jobs today, like app developers, cloud service managers, and SEO specialists, didn't even exist a decade ago, and what will exist five years from now may change as well. The aura surrounding a four-year degree is beginning to lose its sheen, especially if the institution can't ensure that its graduates will end up with a job despite technological disruption. You're just as likely—or more so, in my opinion—to learn more useful skills at a place like Divergence or Udacity than in a four-year degree-granting institution. In the most recent edition of Upwork's Skills Index,[8] none of the top 20 fastest-growing skills required a degree. Fluency with digital workflow platform ServiceNow, cloud service provider Microsoft Azure, open-source deep learning platform PyTorch, and deep learning API Keras, are all skills that can be learned at places like my institution and via fine-tuned apprenticeship programs. Upwork's CEO said that the study confirmed their belief that highly specialized talent need not hail from the Ivy League or other traditional four-year institutions. "Businesses are relying on nontraditional talent sources to effectively engage the best workers, no matter where they live."

What about companies that don't have the right personnel to reskill in the first place? That's when you've got to look at entry-level talent. The talent we train at Divergence is entry-level. Our graduates are the ideal candidates, but unlike many other institutions, we commit to placing our graduates in jobs. How do you place entry-level talent? It's a fundamental building block question. I've made hundreds of calls to corporations and asked CEOs how they're hiring entry-level talent, and invariably, the responses are the same: "We go through campus programs and we hire graduates and give them an opportunity. We give them internships and the opportunity to work with a mentor to get them going with our onboarding and training." And to that, I ask them a question in return:

"If you replaced degreed applicants with degree-less applicants but still recruited new talent as you are today, would you hire an entry-level talent from Divergence?" There's no argument, the answer is yes. These executives know that their talent doesn't need a degree. Entry-level talent can be hired from a vocational school like Divergence. Hiring talent with a theoretical understanding of concepts is fine, but it's not enough—you need workers with the skills for now and for five years from now. That information helped me shape Divergence into the vocational trade school of the twenty-first century, and with further buy-in from companies, I've been routinely successful in placing graduates in entry-level positions at high-demand companies.

CHAPTER EIGHT
Wardens of the Future

The possibility of a worldwide influenza pandemic in the near future is of growing concern for many countries around the globe. Many predictions of the economic and social costs of a modern-day influenza pandemic are based on the effects of the influenza pandemic of 1918.

Thomas A. Garrett, Assistant Vice President and Economist, Federal Reserve Bank of St. Louis, November 2007.

The hope is that, in not too many years, human brains and computing machines will be coupled together very tightly, and that the resulting partnership will think as no human brain has ever thought and process data in a way not approached by the information-handling machines we know today.

J.C.R. Licklider, "Man-Computer Symbiosis" [1960]

In 2005, the World Bank estimated that an influenza pandemic could cost the global economy upwards of $800 billion,[1] while the

U.S. Centers for Disease Control and Prevention calculated that such an event would run $166 billion stateside and kill 207,000 Americans.[2] As we find ourselves in the middle of just such a crisis, these numbers are, sadly, the product of aspirational thinking: as of printing, over 600,000[3] Americans have died due to Covid-19 and the pandemic will likely cost the country $16 trillion, or almost the equivalent of one year's GDP.

Still, at times like these, we can learn from the past in order to build a better future. The last major pandemic in 1918 killed 675,000 Americans. Only the Black Death that ravaged Europe in the 14th century killed more people—an estimated 25 million, over a five-year period. Though sparse, we do have some data from 1918 that reflects how the American economy fared in the wake of the pandemic. Notably, short-term impacts were mostly temporary:

> The Spanish flu left almost no discernible mark on the aggregate US economy. The coronavirus arrived to the US at a time of booming stock market values. By contrast, the influenza outbreak in the spring of 1918 occurred right after a downturn: the Dow Jones Industrial Average had actually declined 21.7% in 1917. Yet the stock market recovered substantially during the pandemic, with the Dow index increasing by 10.5% in 1918 and by 30.5% in 1919. In fact, 1919 stands as the ninth best year for the Dow from 1915 to 2019. According to some estimates, real gross national product actually grew in 1919, albeit by a modest 1% (Romer 1988). In new work, Velde (2020) shows that most indicators of aggregate economic activity suffered modestly, and those that did decline more significantly right after the influenza outbreak, like industrial output,

> recovered within months. That the impact of the influenza pandemic on the aggregate US economy was mild should be surprising.[4]

Additionally, the 1918 flu led to innovations that accelerated the race to modern living: electric dishwashers were touted as helpful gadgets in fighting flu transmission; shoppers were encouraged to place orders and distance learners to conduct their lessons from home using a telephone. Public health initiatives such as increased vaccinations and updating building code requirements to ensure better ventilation were directly shaped by the pandemic.

What kinds of innovation will we see in the post-Covid era? The full extent of the virus's impact on human life and the economy remains to be seen, but it has been a tremendous force for change—change that would have otherwise transpired, but certainly not with the speed that we saw throughout 2020. Briefly, here's a recap of that change and what we need to address in the years to come:

» The digital experience is now fully embedded in daily life. Businesses will need to continue to adapt their digital platforms to enhance the end user's experience. That means creating thriving personalized and interactive virtual communities.

» Human-AI collaboration will only continue to improve, from facilitating the race to a vaccine for Covid-19 to creating chatbots capable of working with humans in extended reality environments, AI will learn and adapt seamlessly to different environments. Further improvements to AI will include natural language processing and greater ease with which humans can understand and code AI systems.

» Over 75 billion connected devices will populate the world by 2025, with a projected market value of $1.1 trillion. Many of these devices will be created in "forever beta" mode, meaning developers will be able to reconfigure the functionality of these items over time. This advance presents tremendous value for customers who, rather than trading in hardware for new iterations, will eventually expect their devices to adapt with the times. Regular updates may leave some end users frustrated and left behind in the digital dust. This so-called "beta burden" will require developers to create flexible application programming interfaces to allow adaptability.

» Robots will proliferate and become further integrated in social and professional spheres. Finding the right way to introduce and integrate robots into the world will require upskilling and retooling for robotics technicians and other scientists.

In sum, rapid advancements in new technologies and maturation of older digital technologies will benefit companies and customers so long as innovation is constant. These developments will require a nimble workforce willing to learn on the go. Business leaders must accept that they are at the forefront of the changes underway, both as innovators ushering in a new era and as disruptors upending current business models.

Any company that adapts quickly—in part by investing in retraining its workforce—will find sizeable opportunities for growth. Consider, for example, the group of tech companies known collectively by the acronym FAANG— Facebook, Apple, Amazon, Netflix, and Google—which together constitute 21 percent of the S&P 500's entire market value. None of these companies existed thirty years ago, and they will likely continue to dominate. The questions, then, are: Will these companies share their value creation with stakeholders, and how will they promote the kind of change necessary for others to succeed? Will these companies recognize the need to maintain a workforce that's constantly learning, and will they be willing to hire talent from non-traditional sources? My sense, as I've discussed throughout this book, is that they will.

Automation is going to eat everybody's lunch, let's not forget that. But also recall that 97 million new jobs will be created in the U.S. by the shift in the labor market towards digital work. These new jobs will require workers to skill up. I learned this when I got laid off as a forty-four-year-old in 2014, but now, workers have to accept that we are each going to have multiple careers in our lifetimes, each requiring different skills. In fact, before I was let go, I ran a project at Microsoft aimed at shepherding IT pros through the new labyrinth of constant digital change in the workforce. Even then, we were preparing, albeit on a micro level, for constant disruption and being ready to meet those changes quickly. A sustainable career does not mean one career, but that a worker can shape-shift to get to where they need to be.

Older generations may have a hard time wrapping their minds around this concept, but I strongly believe that our digitally native generations will find this fact neither cumbersome nor stressful, so long as they are equipped with the tools necessary to succeed in the workplace.

In the current scheme of things, people joining the workforce today should reasonably expect to have anywhere from six to twelve careers in their lifetime, all due to the unending change wrought by digital technologies.

Jobs will come, jobs will go, but there will always be a need for a workforce, and the incessant cycle of hiring and firing workers does not help anyone's bottom line. Staying static is a death sentence. Doing what you did for the last decade will not get you a job in the near future. That's why you need tech-based vocational trade schools to skill people up for the next job. Even at my institute, I make sure that my curricula are updating regularly to prepare our learners for the jobs that will require current skill sets, and my instructors need to be capable of employing technologies like avatars, robots, and holodeck simulations in their coursework. We are at the cusp of that man-computer symbiosis that ARPA scientist J.C.R Licklider coined in his article on the topic.

Ultimately, I think the pandemic forced companies to look inward and ask if they were ready for rapid change, like telecommuting and automating services. Work could not cease entirely, so how could digital technology be harnessed to transform and modernize? Larger companies made the shift more rapidly, but the hundreds of thousands of small businesses were stuck. Small, family-owned restaurants were forced to pivot or they folded. Bistros and cafés that previously maintained a minimal web presence suddenly needed to set up online ordering, streamline inventory management, and accept mobile payments. These systems are likely to remain permanent fixtures in the small business ecosystem, and with a little breathing room, those with the ability to do so will continue to innovate and will thrive as a result.

Once again, the past is prologue: jobs were lost in the early 1990s to cheaper labor overseas, but we adapted. Here we are in the 2020s, and politicians are lobbying to bring those manufacturing jobs back. But those are relics of another era. Yes, bring jobs, but bring innovation with them. Don't tell the American public that coal or steel will be the path to prosperity—they aren't, at least not in their past forms. Industries that will thrive in the United States will require a workforce with a sophisticated understanding of digital technology, and only a vocational technical education will help employees through this process.

In the years to come, you may be a lineman on the factory floor, but the machine you're working on is going to be operated by a robot and you will be on the other side of the factory floor handling the robot. Your job will require a totally different skill set than the one you have now, even if you remain in the same industry where you started out.

I am confident that there are going to be more jobs, in part because our world population is increasing, and we consume a lot. There's nothing wrong with a demand-based society, but we need to be ready to feed it.

I recently participated in a discussion panel for VET TEC, the technology program offered through the Veterans Administration that matches veterans with training providers who teach in-demand tech skills. As it happens, Divergence offers cybersecurity and data science training programs to veterans through VET TEC, and the panel was focused on the importance of building recruiting programs to facilitate the hiring of veterans into companies that need employees with these skills. Fellow panel participants, included representatives from Disney+, Accenture, and Walmart, among others. I was there to talk about how Divergence is both creating opportunities for potential hires and training potential hires for digital-based jobs. My school is paving the way by showing that we can hire apprentices and put them on strategic initiatives related to talent management systems and Divergence Labs, and so can others. My fellow panel participants echoed my sentiments: they want recruits to know Excel, basic structured query language (SQL), and low-code and no-code skills that are becoming the standard in businesses around the world. The programming skills that I learned in the early days of my career are no longer necessary for a productive career as a software technician.

I hope that the roughly eight hundred attendees walked away from that session saying, "I can be part of information technology and be part of automation and drive change." Having representatives from places like Walmart and Disney+ say that they are actively considering hiring from non-traditional programs adds fuel to the fire: there are companies that will hire military veterans with tech credentials from a non-traditional school.

We are empowering individuals to be successful at building sustainable careers and a lifetime of stability—by accepting that change is constant and being prepared for it. This is the "rapid" change that has been in the works for decades. This is not something that was unexpected, it's just whether people have been prepared for it or not. Now there really is no choice. Either you have to prepare or you are going to be in a tough spot.

There are three ingredients I believe everyone needs to possess or cultivate if they're going to have any chance of making it in the new economy: passion, purpose, and progress. You've got to have passion. Have the passion to make a difference, then purpose will come. I think of my path with Divergence. When people ask me if I had a vision, the answer is no. At least, not at the outset. All I wanted to do was survive. I wanted to make a living. I wanted to put food on the table and I put my time and energy into making Divergence succeed. But during the process I found my purpose, which was to find a meaningful way to help people in career transition. Now, seeing Divergence grow has fueled my desire to make more progress, which also requires passion. It is a self-fulfilling cycle and once you're in it, it's hard to undo. Thankfully, the benefits are limitless.

ABOUT DIVERGENCE ACADEMY

Ranked as one of the top-rated and fasted-growing privately held companies in America by Inc.com in 2021, Divergence is a vocational school for the 21st century offering hands on practice with real-time feedback and apprenticeship opportunities in tech-driven industries. Our goal is to empower individuals to not merely survive, but to thrive in the high-speed tech and data-driven economy. Emerging technology can't run itself; it needs living, breathing human beings to keep it running. That means preparing for careers in AI, cloud computing, cybersecurity, statistical analysis, and data science. Non-traditional learners and veterans form the backbone of our student body, and we help place learners at in-demand positions with the potential for long-term growth.

https://divergence.one

ABOUT THE AUTHOR

Sravan Ankaraju understands the pipeline jungles and hidden feedback loops associated with the world of machine learning, having started his career as a developer of large-scale transactional systems applying various tree-based algorithms. His twenty-five years in the field of data science and innovation provided him with a robust understanding of the intersections between technology and the economy.

From 2001 to 2014, Sravan worked at Microsoft as a strategy and innovation leader, where he moved large teams from reactive to predictive to prescriptive support by embracing risk-based assessments and machine learning models.

In 2016, Sravan founded Divergence Academy, where he is responsible for the strategic vision and business development for industry-focused technology education. Divergence Academy offers immersive programs in data science, cyber security, and cloud computing and was ranked one of Inc.com's fastest-growing privately-held companies in America in 2021.

Sravan resides in Texas with his wife, Sangeeta, and their two children.

ENDNOTES

CHAPTER 1: Hope Is Not a Strategy

1 Davis, Michelle. 2019. "JPMorgan Rolls Out Robots to Scrutinize Banker Travel, Expenses." *Bloomberg*, December 11, 2019. https://www.bloomberg.com/news/articles/2019-12-11/jpmorgan-rolls-out-robots-to-scrutinize-banker-travel-expenses

2 Berezoe, Alex. 2020. "Will Artificial Intelligence Replace Pathologists, Radiologists, Microbiologists?" American Council on Science and Heath, August 21, 2020. https://www.acsh.org/news/2020/08/21/will-artificial-intelligence-replace-pathologists-radiologists-microbiologists-14979

3 Semuels, Alana. 2020. "Millions of Americans Have Lost Jobs in the Pandemic—and Robots and AI Are Replacing Them Faster Than Ever." *TIME*, August 6, 2020. https://time.com/5876604/machines-jobs-coronavirus/

CHAPTER 2: The Microsoft Years

1 U.S. Department of Commerce. 1999. "The Economics of Y2K and the Impact on the United States." Economics and Statistics Administration, U.S. Department of Commerce, November 17, 1999. https://www.commerce.gov/sites/default/files/migrated/reports/y2k_1.pdf

2 Ibid, iii.

3 Hollingsworth, Heather. 2020. "Interest in Homeschooling Has 'Exploded Amid Covid-19 Pandemic." *AP News*, August 12, 2020. https://apnews.com/article/health-distance-learning-lifestyle-featured-nebraska-23033c2f23fb1708d2f5b797becb2b0f

CHAPTER 3: Crisis Breeds Opportunity

1 Speak Up. 2016. *From Print to Pixel: The Role of Videos, Games, Animations and Simulations within K-12 Education*. Speak Up, 2016. https://tomorrow.org/speakup/pdfs/Speak%20Up%20May%202015_PR1.pdf

2 Deterding S., Dixon D., Khaled R., et al. 2011. "From Game Design Elements to Gamefulness: Defining Gamification." In: *Proceedings of the 15th International Academic MindTrek Conference: Envisioning Future Media Environments, Tampere, Finland, 28–30 September 2011*, pp.9–15. New York: ACM.

3 Taylor & Francis. 2018. "Checking Phones in Lectures Can Cost Students Half a Grade in Exams." *Phys.org*, July 27, 2018. https://phys.org/news/2018-07-students-grade-exams.html

4 Gottlieb, Scott. 2001. "Surgeons Perform Transatlantic Operation Using Fibreoptics." *BMJ* 2001, no. 323 (September):713 doi:10.1136/bmj.323.7315.713/c

5 https://www.davincisurgery.com/

6 Siegel, Rachel. 2019. "Tweens, Teens and Screens: The Average Time Kids Spend Watching Online Videos Has Doubled in 4 years." *The Washington Post*, October 29, 2019. https://www.washingtonpost.com/technology/2019/10/29/survey-average-time-young-people-spend-watching-videos-mostly-youtube-has-doubled-since/

7 Hill, Phil. 2013. "The Most Thorough Summary (to date) of MOOC Completing Rates." *eLiterate*, February 26, 2013. https://eliterate.us/the-most-thorough-summary-to-date-of-mooc-completion-rates/

CHAPTER 4: Curation Is Greater Than Creation: Bridging the Gap

1 Wiener, Norbert. 1950. *The Human Use of Human Beings*. New York: Houghton Mifflin.

2 Raimonde, Olivie. 2020. "Covid Grows Less Deadly as Doctors Gain Practice, Drugs Improve." *Bloomberg*, September 19, 2020. https://www.bloomberg.com/news/articles/2020-09-19/covid-grows-less-deadly-as-doctors-gain-practice-drugs-improve

3 Goldstein, Dana. 2020. "The Class Divide: Remote Learning at 2 Schools, Private and Public." *The New York Times*, May 9, 2020. https://www.nytimes.com/2020/05/09/us/coronavirus-public-private-school.html

4 Goldstein, Dana. 2020. "Research Shows Students Falling Months Behind During Virus Disruptions." *The New York Times*, June 5, 2020. https://www.nytimes.com/2020/06/05/us/coronavirus-education-lost-learning.html

5 Clarke, Arthur C. 1972. *Profiles of the Future: An Inquiry into the Limits of the Possible.* New York: Bantam Books.

6 Texas Workforce Commission. 2017. "RealPage and Richland College Partner for over $1.3 Million Job-Training Grant." https://www.twc.texas.gov/news/realpage-and-richland-college-partner-over-13-million-job-training-grant

7 Dowd, Maureen. 2017. "Elon Musk's Billion-Dollar Crusade to Stop the A.I. Apocalypse." *Vanity Fair*, April 17, 2017. https://vanityfair.com/news/2017/03/elon-musk-billion-dollar-crusade-to-stop-ai-space-x.

CHAPTER 5: A Virus Accelerates Change

1 Bloom, Nicholas.. "How Working from Home Works Out." *SIEPR Policy Briefs*, June 2020. https://siepr.stanford.edu/research/publications/how-working-home-works-out

2 Paine, John, Steiner, Elizabeth, D., et al. 2017 *How Does Personalized Learning Affect Student Achievement?* RAND Corporation. doi: https://doi.org/10.7249/RB9994

3 Silva, M., Kleinert, W., Sheppard, V., Cantrell, K., et el. 2015. "The Relationship Between Food Security, Housing Stability, and School Performance Among College Students in an Urban University." *Journal of College Student Retention Research Theory and Practice* 19, no. 3 (December). doi:10.1177/1521025115621918

4 https://www.bostondynamics.com/spot

5 Brooks, Rodney. "The Robot Invasion Is Coming—And That's a Good Thing," Discover Magazine, September 2010. https://www.discovermagazine.com/technology/the-robot-invasion-is-comingand-thats-a-good-thing

CHAPTER 6: Speak Softly and Carry a Big Stick

1 Sawhill, Isabel, "What the forgotten Americans really want—and how to give it to them," Brookings, October 2018, https://www.brookings.edu/longform/what-the-forgotten-americans-really-want-and-how-to-give-it-to-them/

2 Frey, Carl B. & Osborne, Michael. (2013). "The Future of Employment: How Susceptible Are Jobs to Computerisation?" *Oxford Martin Programme on Technology & Employment*. Oxford: University of Oxford. https://www.oxfordmartin.ox.ac.uk/downloads/academic/future-of-employment.pdf

3 Stenström, Marja0Leena, and Virolainen, Maarit, "The history of Finnish vocational education and training," Nord-VET—The future of VET in the Nordic Countries, Finnish Institute for Educational Research, 2014, https://www.researchgate.net/profile/Maarit-Virolainen/publication/275798990_The_history_of_Finnish_vocational_education_and_training/links/554716560cf24107d3980f95/The-history-of-Finnish-vocational-education-and-training.pdf

4 Federal Ministry of Education and Research. 2015. *Report on Vocational Education and Training.* https://www.bmbf.de/bmbf/en/education/the-german-vocational-training-system/the-german-vocational-training-system_node.html

5 Ibid.

6 Jacoby, Tamar. 2014. "Why Germany Is So Much Better at Training Its Workers." *The Atlantic*, October 16, 2014. https://www.theatlantic.com/business/archive/2014/10/why-germany-is-so-much-better-at-training-its-workers/381550/

7 Berkowitz, Kelsey. 2019. "Why Do Only a Tiny Fraction of Jobseekers Participate in Registered Apprenticeships?" *Third Way*, November 14, 2019. https://www.thirdway.org/report/why-do-only-a-tiny-fraction-of-jobseekers-participate-in-registered-apprenticeships

8 Fuller, J., Raman, M., et al. 2017. *Dismissed By Degrees*. Published by Accenture, Grads of Life, Harvard Business School. https://www.hbs.edu/managing-the-future-of-work/Documents/dismissed-by-degrees.pdf

CHAPTER 7: Intelligence Amplification

1 Engelbart, Douglas C. 1962. "Augmenting Human Intellect: A Conceptual Framework." *SRI Summary Report* AFOSR-3223. Washington, D.C.: Air Force Office of Scientific Research. https://www.dougengelbart.org/content/view/138

2 Bughin, Jacques, Hazan, Eric, Lund, Susan, et al. 2018. *Skill Shift*. McKinsey Global Institute, May 2018. https://www.mckinsey.com/~/media/mckinsey/industries/public%20and%20social%20sector/our%20insights/skill%20shift%20automation%20and%20the%20future%20of%20the%20workforce/mgi-skill-shift-automation-and-future-of-the-workforce-may-2018.pdf

3 Fuller, Joseph, Raman, Manjari, Bailey, Allison, et al. 2020. "Rethinking the On-Demand Workforce." *Harvard Business Review*, November-December 2020. https://hbr.org/2020/11/rethinking-the-on-demand-workforce

4 Bidwell, Matthew. 2011. "Paying More to Get Less: The Effects of External Hiring versus Internal Mobility." *Administrative Science Quarterly* 56, no. 3 (December): 369-407.

https://knowledge.wharton.upenn.edu/article/why-external-hires-get-paid-more-and-perform-worse-than-internal-staff/

5 Ibid.

6 Cann, Oliver. 2019. "Who Pays for the Reskilling Revolution? Investment to Safeguard America's At-Risk Workers Likely to Cost Government $29 Billion." *WEP News Releases*, January 22, 2019. https://www.weforum.org/press/2019/01/who-pays-for-the-reskilling-revolution-investment-to-safeguard-america-s-at-risk-workers-likely-to-cost-government-29-billion/

7 OECD. 2016. "The State of the North American Labour Market." *Report Prepared for the 2016 North American Leaders Summit*. June 2016. https://www.oecd.org/unitedstates/The-state-of-the-north-american-labour-market-june-2016.pdf

8 https://www.upwork.com/resources/in-demand-jobs-and-skills

CHAPTER 8: Wardens of the Future

1 Brahmbhatt, Milan. 2005. "Avian Influenza: Economic and Social Impacts." The World Bank, Washington, D.C., a speech delivered Sept. 23, 2005.

2 https://www.cdc.gov/flu/about/burden/index.html

3 https://covid.cdc.gov/covid-data-tracker/#datatracker-home

4 Efraim Benmelech, Carola Frydman, "The 1918 Influenza Did Not Kill the U.S. Economy," *VoxEu CEPR*, April 29, 2020, https://voxeu.org/article/1918-influenza-did-not-kill-us-economy

www.ingramcontent.com/pod-product-compliance
Lightning Source LLC
Chambersburg PA
CBHW030521210326
41597CB00013B/987
9781737776109